CORE
HANDBOOK

10 THINGS EVERY CORE MEMBER SHOULD KNOW

LEADING TEENS CLOSER
TO CHRIST

The information contained herein is published and produced by Life Teen, Inc. The resources and practices are in full accordance with the Roman Catholic Church. The Life Teen® name and associated logos are trademarks registered with the United States Patent and Trademark Office. Use of the Life Teen® trademarks without prior permission is forbidden. Permission may be requested by contacting Life Teen, Inc. at 480-820-7001.

Our sincere thanks to all who contributed to this piece in its original form. A special thanks to the Parish Outreach Team.

Cover design & interior layout by Laura Womack and Casey Olson.

Copy editing by Natalie Tansill and Danielle Rzepka.

Published by Life Teen, Inc.
2222 S. Dobson Rd.
Suite 601
Mesa, AZ 85202
LifeTeen.com

Printed in the United States of America.
Printed on acid-free paper.

For more information about Life Teen or to order additional copies, go online to LifeTeen.com or call us at 1-800-809-3902.

TABLE OF CONTENTS

INTRODUCTION

BY RANDY RAUS

- -

On behalf of the Life Teen Movement, thank you for being a Core Member at your parish. In the past 20 plus years of my youth ministry experience, my absolute favorite role was that of a Core Member. The day to day interaction with young people and relational ministry dynamic always left me feeling that no matter how much I tried to serve teens, God was never outdone in His generosity to me. The more you give in youth ministry, somehow it comes back to you many fold. It is our prayer that this life-giving ministry to, for, and with teenagers will not only transform the lives of the young people you serve but will also transform your life.

Life Teen is a movement of the Holy Spirit in the Catholic Church. Our mission is clear – Life Teen leads teens closer to Christ. As a Core Member, you are on the front lines of this mission everyday. Your example, love, faith, and outreach to young people are a primary way that young people are led closer to Christ.

So what you have signed up to do is to help your parish lead teens closer to Christ. That is the "what?" of our mission. But "why?" is this so important? Because when a teen encounters Christ, it changes *everything*. It changes how active they are in their faith; it changes their friends, their families, their parish, their school, and their world. Our primary task is journeying with young people and setting the environment for them to have an encounter with Christ.

As a Core Member, you are part of a team of people reaching out to teens in your community. The most efficient way to get teens to relate to you is for you to remain authentic at all times. Teens are drawn to people who are authentic and who care more about them than themselves.

This Core Handbook will equip you with the essentials for being a great Core Member. Please know that our entire staff prays for your mission with teens at your parish. We are thankful that you have said "yes" to God in serving His young Church.

Peace,

Randy Raus

Randy Raus
Life Teen President/CEO

ABOUT LIFE TEEN

LEADING TEENS CLOSER
TO CHRIST

GET TO KNOW THE MOVEMENT

BY MATT SMITH

- -

When I started middle school, I was stressed and overwhelmed. In addition to dealing with new drama with the girls, I was getting drama in the classroom. Every teacher expected us to have a notebook just for that class and they had multiple handouts every day. My backpack was heavier than ever, and it was an absolute mess of papers, books, and homework. I was 12 years old, and my little world was spinning around. Then one day my mom bought me a *Trapper Keeper*. Now I had a place to keep ruled paper, handouts, flash cards, and my pencils too. It was magical, and I loved it. It was a simple solution to a complicated problem.

As an adult, I get thrilled when I find simple solutions to complicated problems. These solutions are more rare in our complex world, but they are still there. For example, Christian missionaries in Africa now focus primarily on providing clean water to the communities they minister to.

Why clean water? Because with clean water and better sanitation, a whole litany of moral and societal problems can go away. With a clean water well, children stay close to home and are no longer vulnerable to attacks while on their long journey to retrieve clean water for their thirsty families. Not only can the children be safer, they now have the time to stay in the classrooms and do their homework. And with fewer water-born illnesses, the children miss fewer days of school. And finally, with a stronger education, the children can escape vicious cycles of poverty. They can go on to provide a better economy for their community and their nation. All that goodness from a little water well at the village.

I believe that a simple solution to many, many of the problems our world faces today is **youth ministry**. It sounds almost silly to place all those words next to each other in a sentence. Aren't world problems supposed to be solved by heads of states, or the United Nations? Yes, their work matters, but it will never be enough.

What you do as a Life Teen Core Team at your parish is very important. Quite simply, when you allow Christ to transform the lives of teens, you transform parishes and you begin to transform culture.

Life Teen may have began as a model for how youth ministry is done in our Catholic Church, but it's clear that God was doing more. That is why, in 2006, we prayerfully changed how we describe ourselves. Life Teen is now a **Movement of the Holy Spirit** that is igniting our Catholic faith in communities around the world.

So how does this all apply to what you do as a member of your parish's Core Team? That's a question that we'll answer through each part of this book. But let's first start by defining the five pillars of Life Teen at every parish.

PILLAR 1: THE EUCHARIST
Because sacramental spirituality is the only spirituality that lasts.

We believe that an engaging, reverent youth liturgy changes the lives of teenagers at a parish. Other models of youth ministry focus on social events, sports, or service; but with Life Teen, the Catholic Mass remains central. Much will change in the lives of teenagers, but their connection to Christ through the Eucharist will always stay the same.

This fosters lifelong vocations within our Church. In a 2010 survey, the USCCB Office of Vocations found that 49 percent of current U.S. seminarians were involved in Life Teen when they were in high school. That's remarkable considering that Edge and Life Teen ministries are only implemented in 8.3 percent of U.S. parishes. There are also some Life Teen graduates that are now elected officials in the U.S. Congress and are fighting for a Culture of Life.

PILLAR 2: RELATIONAL MINISTRY
Because teens don't care what you have to say until they know that you care.

In the Life Teen model of youth ministry, a youth minister, priest, and Core Team of adults form a discipleship team that builds relationships with young people in their parish community. In the beginning, these strong relationships will help build your youth program; but ultimately, these relationships will open teens' hearts to the Gospel.

PILLAR 3: EVANGELIZATION AND CATECHESIS
Because when you go where teens are, you know how to speak the Truth into their lives.

Everyone deserves the chance to hear the Gospel, not just the teenagers already sitting in your church pews. That's why Life Teen encourages youth ministers and their Core Teams to get out of the parish and into the community to invite teenagers to Mass and Life Night.

We've found that teens are more eager to learn about the Faith when they are out of the classroom and with their friends in a large group. We believe in sharing the timeless Truth in a timely way. That's why our Edge Nights and Life Nights are inviting, exciting, and engaging. We teach the fullness of the Catholic faith, plus we give young people answers to their questions about current issues with their families, at school, and in the world.

PILLAR 4: ENCOUNTER
Because teens don't just want to know about Christ. They want to know Christ Himself.

It's easy to make Jesus impersonal. It's easy to focus on programming, schedules, and calendars in youth ministry. But we can never forget why we do this: to direct teenagers into a personal relationship with Christ. Everything we do in Life Teen – liturgies, weekly gatherings, retreats – should lead to giving teens an opportunity to encounter the Living God.

Edge and Life Teen parishes also have a distinct Marian spirituality. We have seen that teens are drawn closer to Christ through Mary's example and her intercession.

PILLAR 5: CONNECTING TO THE MOVEMENT
Because young people need to know that they're not alone.

When a parish implements Life Teen, teens can take their Catholic identity to a deeper level by connecting to the entire Life Teen Movement. It could be as simple as having an XLT night of prayer once a month with nearby parishes. Or parishes can bring their teens to take part in any of our regional youth events, summer conferences, or summer camps. Core Teams can come to any our training conferences. Get your teens connected to LifeTeen.com, the world's largest website for Catholic youth.

So how does this all apply to what you do as a member of your parish's Core Team? That's a question that we'll answer through each chapter of this book. More importantly, enjoy this chapter of your life as a Core Member.

LIFE TEEN AS A RESOURCE FOR YOU

BY RANDY RAUS

- -

Once upon a time, the word "blog" brought to mind images of a digital version of a teenage girl's diary — with little value for a large audience. Today there are over 150 million blogs covering everything from personal diaries to informational, instructional, or inspirational content on specialized topics. At Life Teen, our websites offer blogs specifically for teens and also blogs for youth leaders, especially Core Members.

New blogs for youth leaders are posted almost daily on Life Teen's CatholicYouthMinistry.com. These blogs range in topics from how to get more teens to attend an event to ways to lead small groups. It also includes blogs that give you steps to improving your own personal prayer life. All of our blogs are geared to real-life youth ministry situations with the goal of inspiring youth leaders to become more effective in the ministry they serve. There is always something new and inspiring to read in our blogs. As a Core Member it is critical to continue growing in knowledge of this vital ministry. Life Teen blogs are fantastic resources to connect you with the latest in Catholic youth ministry today.

The best way to make the most of reading blogs is to write down the top things you want to remember and discuss them with another Core Member or with your youth minister. Come up with a plan on how you are going to apply the ideas in the blog to your ministry with teens or to your own personal prayer life. Once you have made a plan, then it's time to put the plan into practice within the ministry you serve.

CAMPS AND CONFERENCES

BY CHRIS TURNER

- -

Each year, over 2,000 youth ministry leaders receive practical training and spiritual renewal at our adult training conferences. Another 300 adults attend one of our adult retreats. Almost 7,000 teens have their faith come alive at a summer youth conference. 4,000 teens and middle school youth will have their "best week ever!" at one of our Edge or Life Teen Summer Camps. As Core Members, you have the opportunity to experience all of these!

Why does it matter? Why do we do all of these events all over the world? The reason is simple, but the impact is significant. When a person encounters Jesus Christ in the Church, it changes everything. For adults, it changes how they do youth ministry; it also changes how they interact with their kids, their spouses, and their co-workers. When teens encounter Christ, their lives will never be the same. Relationships become focused on Christ. Prayer becomes a cornerstone in their lives and going to Mass becomes the highlight of their week. All of this starts and is strengthened by an encounter with Jesus Christ.

Take a look at the different types of events we offer:

ADULT TRAINING CONFERENCES
Each year, Life Teen hosts national training conferences for youth ministry leaders (including Core Members). These trainings focus on two things: practical training and spiritual renewal. Our desire is for youth leaders to leave these events on fire for Christ and ready to tackle youth ministry

at their parish. In addition, we host a series of one-day trainings, called "Empower," specifically designed for Core Members. These events feature many of the training topics of a national training conference, but in a more convenient location and time frame.

- Catholic Youth Ministry Training Convention
- Regional Life Teen Training Conferences
- Select International Training Conferences
- Edge and Life Teen Empowers

ADULT RETREATS
Several times each year, Life Teen offers a series of adult retreats at Camp Covecrest, our camp and retreat facility in Northern Georgia. These retreats are designed to renew and refresh the faith walk of adults, whether they are involved in youth ministry or not. All of the details are taken care of so that those who attend can more fully enter into the retreat. Many of our retreat guests make these events a tradition each year.

- Life Teen Men's Retreat
- Life Teen Women's Retreat
- Life Teen Musician's Training Retreat

TEEN EVENTS
The heart of Life Teen is its mission of leading teens closer to Christ. Through teen events, we are able to see this mission in action as hearts are transformed and a generation is given an opportunity to fall in love with the Church. The Life Teen Leadership Conference hosts over 500 high school juniors and seniors each summer and invites them to take their faith to the next level through service and leadership — all flowing from a deep love of the Lord. At a weekend conference, like our Steubenville Youth Conferences, thousands of teens experience Christ in a new and profound way through relevant speakers, powerful music,

and the Sacraments. Even with our one-day rally events, the mission of leading teens closer to Christ remains the same.

- Life Teen Leadership Conference
- Steubenville Youth Conferences hosted by Life Teen
- Inspiration Rallies

EDGE AND LIFE TEEN SUMMER CAMP
We use the phrase "best week ever!" to describe a week at one of our three summer camps. Teens and youth may have loved the idea of the mud pit or the day spent whitewater rafting. They may have signed up to go high in the sky on the high ropes course. Or they may have been attracted to coming to camp simply to hang out with their friends. However, by the end of the week, when campers are asked what the highlights of their week were, their answers are always centered on God. Experiences like daily Mass, Eucharistic Adoration, and the Sacrament of Reconciliation are central to a week of camp. Core Members have an entire week to journey with their teens — in both the serious and the silly moments. Plus, we've assembled a dream team of summer missionaries, priests, hosts, and musicians who make it a priority to spend time with parishes. Summer camp is an incredible way to jump start parish youth ministry for the next year.

- Edge Camp Hiawassee
- Life Teen Camp Covecrest
- Edge and Life Teen Camp Tepeyac

LIFETEEN.COM/EVENTS
We are always improving and innovating our events, retreats, and conferences. Be sure to check out lifeteen. com/events to see what new and exciting opportunities are in store for you and your parish!

2

CORE SPIRITUALITY

BY MARK HART

FIRST THINGS FIRST: THE "SPIRITUALITY" OF LIFE TEEN

- -

Is there urgency to your prayer life?

If I were to offer you one dollar to email me with your address, would you accept the offer and do so? Would you take the time to email for such a minimal amount of money?

What if I offered you fifty dollars - no strings attached - to email me your mailing address? Again, if you knew me, knew I was not scamming you and that it was completely out of the kindness of my *obviously* benevolent heart... would you do it? Okay, what if I offered you one thousand dollars? Would that be enough of an incentive for you to write me?

Now, what if I offered you fifty thousand or one hundred thousand dollars? What if I offered you one million dollars to email me your address?

For anyone reading this who trusted in the offer and believed it to be legit, the number of people who'd actually write in would undoubtedly grow as the worth of the prize grew. It's basic human logic. **The urgency we assign to something is directly proportional to the value we place upon it.**

Now, apply that same principle to your daily prayer life. How much time and effort do you put into your personal prayer time? If prayer and - by extension - if our relationship with God is primary in our life, then it will show in the urgency and primacy we place upon it.

This exercise isn't intended to make any of us feel bad. We can all improve our prayer lives. It is designed, however, to help us take a realistic inventory of the role prayer does (or ought to) play in our lives.

If you're going to serve in youth ministry, your effectiveness and ultimate joy will be directly correlated to how strong your prayer life is and continues to become. Prayer isn't optional when working in ministry, especially when working with the young Church that is beset on all sides by the lies and lures of our painfully self-focused, modern culture. Our teens are the future saints of our Church and they need saints-in-training (you and I) to be their mentors on this moral battlefield they're making their way through.

In accepting this challenge to serve in youth ministry, you are accepting God's battle plan for their (and your) salvation, and that battle plan requires great discipline and sacrifice on your part. The question is not "How strong is your prayer life currently?" but, rather, "How strongly are you dedicated to your daily prayer life becoming?"

If we want our relationship with God to become its strongest, we must allow the Holy Spirit to begin with the areas that we are weakest.

If you want to see where your heart really is, pay attention to where your mind goes when it wanders. The truth that Christ gave us in Matthew 6:21 is as poignant, practical, and timeless as anything in the Gospels; it pierces our souls just as directly in the 21st century as it did in the 1st.

> *"For where your treasure is, there also will your heart be."*
> *– Matthew 6:21*

Commit this verse to memory and make the commitment, today, to identify the areas of your life most in need of spiritual fine-tuning or overhaul, and invite the Holy Spirit to go to work on you.

BEING > DOING

This Core Handbook from Life Teen is filled with practical insight on how to be a "successful" Core Member. Pay attention to the ideas and implement them fully. They're based on decades of experience from people who interact with teens daily.

That being said, you can only properly "do" after you've taken time in prayer...only then will your ministry (actually, God's ministry through you) be rightly ordered. While Shakespeare offered, "To be or not to be," the more important question in the spiritual life is, "Is it better to be or to do?"

Do you remember the story of Martha and Mary? Of course you do...every good Catholic has heard at least one homily in their lifetime praising Mary who sat at the Lord's feet while her sister Martha (patron saint of waiters and waitresses... true story) scurries around waiting on Jesus.

Let's have another look:
> *"Now as they went on their way, he entered a village; and a woman named Martha received him into her house. And she had a sister called Mary, who sat at the Lord's feet and listened to his teaching. But Martha was distracted with much serving; and she went to him and said, "Lord, do you not care that my sister has left me to serve alone? Tell her then to help me." But the Lord answered her, "Martha, Martha, you are anxious and troubled about many things; one thing is needful. Mary has chosen the good portion, which shall not be taken away from her." - Luke 10:38-42*

Now, Martha often gets a pretty bad rap. What was she doing wrong? She was serving the Lord - Martha's "love language" was "acts of service." Her hospitality is how St.

Martha showed her love for God. Truth be told, hospitality was actually the foundation of the entire Mediterranean culture in Jesus' time - it was the highest expectation and form of love in the mind of many. You'll find this mindset on many Core Teams...Core Members who are far more comfortable "doing" than praying, serving than "being." It's the great challenge of the Christian life, especially for leaders. It's easier to love others in the name of Christ than it is to just sit and be loved by Christ in our daily prayer time.

This is where control freaks (like myself) come unraveled. It's far easier for me to show my love for my wife through accomplishing a list of tasks than for me to just sit on the couch and be "present" to her for long conversations. As the groom, it's a constant, daily struggle for me to just slow down and share space with my bride.

The exact opposite is true of Christ, the bridegroom. He is constantly present, ever available to His bride, the Church. He is waiting and desiring the most intimate relationship possible with each and every one of us. His presence in the Eucharist is an invitation to prayer, and more to the point, to intimacy.

During his visit to Australia for World Youth Day in 2008, Pope Emeritus Benedict XVI expounded upon this concept that we must first "be" (receive Christ) before we can "do" (offer Christ):

"These gifts of the Spirit – each of which, as Saint Francis de Sales reminds us, is a way to participate in the one love of God – are neither prizes nor rewards. They are freely given (cf. 1 Cor 12:11). And they require only one response on the part of the receiver: I accept! **Here we sense something of the deep mystery of being Christian. What constitutes our faith is not primarily what we do but what we receive.** *After all, many generous people who are not Christian may well achieve*

far more than we do. Friends, do you accept being drawn into God's Trinitarian life? Do you accept being drawn into his communion of love?"- Pope Benedict XVI

Do you see what he said there? This is more than just saying, "You can't give what you don't have." In essence, this is him saying, "It's better to receive than to give," or more to the point, to be a true Christian, it's a necessity to receive Christ and the gifts of the Spirit, if you desire to give to others... otherwise our giving will be dis-ordered.

Anyone can serve the poor. Atheists can be far more benevolent than many Christians. What makes us Christian is the "why" we do it - the "Who" we do it for and the "Who" that empowers us to serve!

If we show up to serve on Core but haven't prayed, it's not really God that we're doing it for...it's not glorifying the Holy Trinity of Father, Son, and Spirit as much as it an exercise of praise for the minor trinity of me, myself, and I.

When we pray, however, and when we consistently seek Jesus in the Sacraments, most specifically in the Eucharist through Mass and Adoration, all of our acts of service in our homes, schools, offices, and especially on the Core Team now flow from our interior prayer life and are, thus, rightly ordered. In short, our doing (at Life Nights) will be truly pure because it will be in a response to our be-ing (prayer).

GETTING PRACTICAL
So, once we've mastered the art of "be-ing" (and not a moment sooner, Martha), what can you "do" to become more Eucharistic in your spirituality?

Allow me to suggest several ideas that continue to help me:

1. **Commit to a daily Eucharistic encounter with God.** While daily Mass is optimal, it may not be possible for you due to distance, employment hours, school schedule, or other variables out of your control. Perhaps it is possible, though, and you just need to rearrange your sleep or life schedule. Do whatever you can to make it to a daily Mass, or at the very least, Mass during the week beyond just Sundays. The Eucharist is the hinge pin to your faith; it is the axle without which the wheels of your spiritual life will eventually come off. Get to Mass as frequently as possible, and when not possible, find a chapel and get yourself to adoration of the Blessed Sacrament.

2. **'Fess up.** Consider how often you get to Confession and then double it. A good rule of thumb is to get to Confession at least once a month if not twice a month. Out of the gate you may even want to go weekly. The more you go, the more grace you'll have to do battle against the serious sins in your life. Grace builds on grace, and the more frequently you avail yourself of the Sacrament, the more you will want to do so.

3. **Make every day Mother's Day.** When Jesus gave us His blessed mother from the cross (John 19), He offered us all an invaluable invitation to grow closer to Him in intimacy. Mary is the means by which we will grow most perfectly in our discipleship; her guidance, intercession, and protection are unrivaled. The more Marian we become, the more Christian we will become. Invite the Blessed Virgin to pray with you every time you make the sign of the cross. Recommit to the rosary - daily, if possible - for by it we grow in our contemplative prayer life and our love for the Lord. The rosary is the greatest Bible study you'll ever pray.

4. **Word! Speaking of the Bible...how Catholic are you?** We often joke about our Biblical illiteracy as Catholics but why should we? Do we realize that the Catholic Church gave the world the Bible in its unedited form? Praise be to God for this precious family heirloom. Dust off the gift of Scripture, literally and figuratively. Commit to reading the daily readings. Learn the art of lectio divina (check out LifeTeen.com for the "how" to do it). Begin (or continue) to pray the Liturgy of the Hours. Get more into the Word of God (Christ) by getting into His Words (the Bible).

5. **Read any good books lately?** In addition to reading Scripture daily, commit to having at least one spiritual work, Catholic classic or other solidly Catholic book you're reading at the same time. You'll grow not only in knowledge and in faith, but in discipline. The more tools you arm yourself with as a Core Member, the more the Holy Spirit will have to work with!

6. **Stop and ask for directions.** Do you have a spiritual director? If so, go more frequently. If not, get one as soon as possible. Can't find one? Ask around until you find one. And in the interim continue your spiritual readings.

7. **Run away.** You're a soldier for Christ... now *retreat!* As in, go on a personal retreat annually if not more. Get away from the noise, the work, and the stress. Get away and allow the Lord to speak to you, to refill you, and to love on you in an environment where He doesn't have to fight for your attention.

8. **Never stop training.** After they were named "apostles" (which means "sent") the twelve didn't stop being disciples (which means "student"). They kept sitting at Jesus' feet. They kept learning and growing. Get to Training Conferences either sponsored by Life Teen or by your diocese. Look for ways to sharpen your skills and to grow

in knowledge. The more we learn and humble ourselves to grow, the more our prayer life, too, will broaden.

Implement these ideas as soon as you can and watch your prayer life continue to blossom in ways you could never achieve on your own.

THE HEART OF THE MATTER

One final thought: talking about the "spirituality" of Life Teen is really talking about the heart of youth ministry, the heart of a Core Member. The term spirituality doesn't refer to a theology as much as it does a life rightly ordered to God. It refers to how a Catholic should function, deepen, live, and act. As a Core Member, you should be a living embodiment of what it means to live and act as a Catholic Christian in the modern age. People should be able to look at your prayer life, your home life, your work, and school life and say to themselves, "That's the type of man or woman I am called to become and that I aspire to be."

As a fan of etymology (the study of the origin of words), it's ironic to note that the Latin word for heart is "cor"...we see its derivative in Italian (*cuore*), Spanish (*corazon*), and French (*couer*), to name a few. Put simply, Core means "heart," and at the parish, you are the heart of the youth ministries—not just the backbone. For that reason, we must look to our Blessed Mother for her prayerful intercession and wisdom.

In the larger Body of Christ that is the Church, the Holy Spirit is the soul and Mary is the heartbeat. Life Teen is dedicated and consecrated to Mary. We look to her for everything, trusting that the deepest intimacy with Christ is only possible through her immaculate intercession.

The Immaculate Heart of Mary leads us to Christ in ways we cannot achieve on our own.

Pray with Mary, daily. Ask her to pray with and for you, constantly. You will begin to see your life consumed, as hers was, with God's grace. It will bring more joy, peace, and (yes) sorrow than you could ever expect, while leading you into the very "core" of God. Indeed, Mary's Immaculate Heart will lead you directly into Jesus' Most Sacred Heart.

Like Mary, your heart, too, will be pierced. Your heart, too, will be challenged to let go of situations that are out of your control. Your heart, too, will be moved by the needs of others and prompt your prayerful intercession.

You, too, will be blessed enough to hold Christ in your hands, at every single Mass. You, too, will consume Christ into your very being, becoming a walking tabernacle, just like Mary. You, too, will be called to offer a humble and hope-filled example to all who God brings before you, just as she did.

In the pages to follow in this Core Handbook and in the years to follow in ministry, seek intense intimacy over solely theology, seek true penitence over mere practicality, seek daily humility over everything else. In doing so, you are seeking the heart of Christ, that is, the heart of a Core Member.

> *"Yet there too you shall seek the Lord, your God; and you shall indeed find him when you search after him with your whole heart and your whole soul." - Deuteronomy 4:29*

THE CORE OF THE MATTER:

1. What is your favorite form of prayer and why?

_____

_____

_____

_____

_____

2. How would you currently rate your prayer life on a scale of 1 to 10? And how can we, as a Core Team, help you improve?

_____

_____

_____

_____

_____

3. Have a discussion as a Core Team on discerning and defining one or two things that you all would agree to do as an ongoing rhythm of prayer. Be realistic, practical, and if necessary, creative.

3

CORE IDENTITY

BY TRICIA TEMBREULL

WHAT IS A CORE MEMBER?

A question I am consistently asked by youth ministers (and, let's be honest, potential Core Members) is, "what is a Core Member?" I don't like using the word "volunteer" because, in truth, it's not an accurate definition. Every single Catholic Christian is called to respond to their Baptismal call. We, the Baptized, are called to "'profess before men the faith (we) have received from God through the Church' and participate in the apostolic and missionary activity of the People of God" (*CCC* 1270).

As a Core Member, you will be asked to answer your baptismal call by serving high school teens as a relational minister, youth minister, and catechist — witnessing your faith through your current vocation or state of life. Your identity, however, is not in what you do as a Core Member, but rather, who you are in the eyes of your Creator. Who you are is a son or daughter (a child) of God. This is what we first want to explore as we help define what it means to be a Core Member.

CHILD OF GOD

Anyone who is a parent or has interacted with a toddler recently knows they can be a handful. They have endless amounts of energy and strong imaginations. They are fearless, and they see everyone as someone to love, not hate. Children don't have jobs, and they rely on adults to provide everything they need, including their boundaries, food, shelter, clothing, and more. Unless adults neglect or harm them, children have no need to worry or fear.

Imagine that freedom and you will discover what it means to be a child of God. To be a child of God, we must embrace some childlike dispositions in order to grow in trust, wisdom, and strength. Not only will this make us better Core Members, it will also make us better disciples of Christ.

Here are some things that we can learn from children:

CHILDREN NAP
As a kid, the last thing you wanted to do was take a nap; however, as adults we would gladly start a petition at work or school for naptime. When you commit to being on Core, you will find that your weeknights and weekends will encompass time doing relational ministry around town as well as at church. Remember to schedule a day of rest so you have balance between family, work, and your tithe of time and talent.

CHILDREN GO TO SCHOOL
It took centuries for you to master the English language or Algebra — who knows, you might still be mastering one or both of them. Whether you have a high school diploma or

a doctorate degree, you are called to continue learning and opening yourself to the promptings of God. In regard to Catholicism, you could read every book in the Vatican library and you still wouldn't know everything about God and His Bride, the Church. As Core, you must be willing to continue gaining knowledge of your Catholic faith and pass on your wisdom to the teens through small group sharing, personal testimony, and at times, the Proclaim of a Life Night.

CHILDREN ARE GIVEN BOUNDARIES
Boundaries and rules provide safety for children to grow mentally, spiritually, and physically. As Core, your local Diocese or Archdiocese and civil authority provide boundaries to protect not only you, but also the teens. Beyond the "safe environment" guidelines, we ask that you follow the commandments God gave His Church so you may be in full communion with the Church. Teens need us to witness our faith 24-hours a day in every relationship, at our workplace, and even on our Facebook walls so that the joy of living out our faith is emphasized within the boundaries that were given by God.

CHILDREN ASK FOR HELP
The older we get, the more we think we can handle everything; and for some reason we stop asking for help. If kids do one thing well, it's asking for help. Questions like why and how are asked out of curiosity and growth, but also dependence on whom they are asking. To be more childlike we need to be able to ask for help and lean on the community God provides us. Asking for help is not a sign of weakness or inability; rather, it's a sign of strength in knowing our gifts and talents and also encourages others to share theirs. Recognize your limits and ask for assistance or resources for Life Nights, retreats, or various pastoral issues that come up in your ministry.

CHILDREN TRUST

I find it fascinating that you never see Jesus scolding His apostles in Scripture, saying, "Don't question me!" He actually encouraged questions to help build trust with His apostles. He never forced anyone to get in the boat or break bread with Him and, at the same time, He never did anything to place His apostles in harm. In personal relationships, trust is broken time and time again. How we heal from these wounds directly affects our intimacy with God, our fellow Core Members, and teens. Children have an ability to trust that allows them to be vulnerable and inclusive of everyone. It may not be easy, but it's necessary to trust not only God but also the teens and Core we serve alongside.

CHILDREN PLAY

To be a child of God you must have time for play. When we get to adulthood, we lose the gift of simply wasting time, picking up a guitar and jamming with friends, going to a movie or the local playground. Whatever is fun and allows you to be creative, carefree, and playful is something you need to find time for. One last thing: don't feel guilty; God, your Father, wants to play too.

THE CORE OF THE MATTER:

1. Which of these aforementioned attributes of a child comes easiest to you?

_____

_____

_____

_____

_____

_____

2. Which, if any, do you sometimes struggle with? Explain.

_____

_____

_____

_____

_____

_____

WHAT DOES THE TITLE "CORE MEMBER" MEAN?

I want you to think about your family right now. Think of your cousins, parents, siblings, uncles and aunts, nieces and nephews, and even your in-laws. Think of their individual personalities, ages, political and religious views, discipline (or lack of discipline), gifts, and talents. Let's face it, there are family members you love to be with and some you avoid at all costs. However, you are family and you take the good with the bad (most of the time), the functional with the dysfunctional.

When I think of a Core Team I think of a dysfunctional parish family that functions for the sake of the teens. I'm not saying this in a bad way, nor am I justifying laziness or dysfunctional behavior among Core Members. Just like with your immediate family, there is not a Core Team that is perfect. Why? Because it is filled with imperfect Core Members with different personalities, ages, ethnic backgrounds, talents, and theological understandings. What makes Core Teams work is that each Core Member strives for personal holiness. The most vibrant Core Teams are filled with unusual combinations of Core Members who unite for a common mission: to lead teens closer to Christ. They accomplish this mission as relational ministers, catechists, and youth ministers.

RELATIONAL MINISTER

There is one thing you must know about teenagers if you are going to be ministering to them: relationships are everything. In the 1960's family and school were the leading

29

influencers of teens. In the 1980's friends and peers moved to the top, and since the year 2000 media, along with friends and peers, are the top three influencers. This is why Life Teen places a large emphasis on relational ministry.

Relational ministry really is a call to evangelize the teens by reaching them where they are emotionally, spiritually, and physically. Like St. Paul, we are called to enter their culture (not reject it) and build relationships with teens centered on Christ that point out the Christian elements within the culture.

As a Core Member you will be asked to participate in evangelization and relational ministry opportunities such as sporting events, hang outs at the local Starbucks, or attending the school musical or talent show. The point of these relational ministry opportunities is to build relationships with the teens where they are most comfortable, confident, and themselves. Seeing teens in their environment will allow you to minister to them honestly and see how they interact with peers. Taking personal time to be in their lives where they least expect an adult to enter will build trust and unity that will allow them to ask the tough questions at a Life Night and approach you when things are not perfect in their personal or faith life.

CATECHIST

When I first started out in youth ministry I taught a Confirmation class with my mom. I realized that there was a lot that I didn't know, and whenever there was a lesson I didn't feel strong teaching, I would try and pass it off to my mom. Well, there was a reason I didn't know the teaching: my mom didn't know it all that well either (parents really are the primary Catechists). However, instead of passing off the teaching, it forced me to start learning new things about my Catholic faith and become a catechist, not just the cool college student that could relate to the teens.

Passing on Church teachings to our teens is the role of a catechist. Life Teen provides you with amazing resources and Proclaim teachings to create powerful Life Nights, retreats, Bible studies, and more. The conviction and knowledge you bring to each night is invaluable in introducing light and life into what Blessed Pope John Paul II called the "culture of death." Combined with the trust that stems from the relational ministry and witness you provide, you have the ability to present truth to a culture that finds truth relative. Dig deep in learning as much as you can about the Life Night topics and realize how much God still wants to catechize and form you.

YOUTH MINISTER

I know what you're thinking: you are the Core Member, not the youth minister... right? Well, sorry to burst your bubble, but if you are a Core Member you are ministering to high school youth and that basically makes you a youth minister. Sure, you might not have to attend the staff meetings or book the hall or retreat centers, but you are still a baptized Catholic who has chosen the apostolate of ministering to the youth of your parish. So what does this mean and what have you really said yes to?

Well, it means you have said yes to living out your Catholic faith and witnessing that faith not only to the teens, but also to everyone you know. It means that you are willing to mentor and hold teens accountable to the faith in which they have been baptized and confirmed. It means that you will protect the teens from harm as your diocese mandates you through safe environment training. It means that you will prepare Life Nights, attend retreats, fully, consciously, and actively participate in Mass on a weekly basis, and share your time, talent, and treasure with the teens. It means you will be the best Catholic Christian you can be and practice what you preach behind closed doors and on the microphone at a Life Night.

THE CORE OF THE MATTER:

1. What elements of relational ministry give you the most anxiety?

_____

_____

_____

_____

2. What can you do to deepen your own knowledge as a catechist?

_____

_____

_____

_____

3. Do you think of yourself as a youth minister, why or why not? Please explain.

_____

_____

_____

_____

PRIMARY VOCATION

One of Life Teen's most challenging Core Values is to uphold your primary vocation. So, what is a primary vocation? I'm going to make it simple: to love God. The word vocation comes from the Latin *vocatio*, which means to summon, or *vocare*, which means to call. A call, however, means nothing when we fail to pick up, listen, and respond. The same is true when God commands us to love. We must pick up, listen, and respond to His call to "love one another" (John 13:38).

We are all called to love (*CCC* 1604, 2331), and the way each of us is called to love one another through the Sacraments of the Church is personal and profound. Let's explore two vocations (marriage and holy orders) and one state of life (single) to see how we can best live out our vocations to the fullest and keep them primary in our life.

MARRIAGE

When I was younger, my mom and dad were very involved in the Marriage Encounter movement. My mom would make phone calls to couples constantly. I remember vividly an afternoon at the kitchen table doing my homework when my sister wanted my mom's attention. My mom was on the phone and my sister shouted, "You love that phone more than you love me!" My mom immediately put down the receiver, welled up in tears, and proceeded to help my sister. There was truth in my sister's outcry and my mom knew it. She was out of order, and I'm not talking about my sister's words; I'm talking about my mom's primary vocation.

If you are married, your marriage is your priority. If only one of you is committed to Core, make sure the other doesn't become a "ministry widow." I have seen marriages suffer from spouses feeling abandoned for ministry. Ministry cannot be an escape for what's going wrong at home either. You must work at your marriage more than you work at being a great Core Member, and if you are having spousal issues, don't avoid them; confront them and seek healing.

Your apostolate must flow from your vocation, not vice versa. Communication is essential for any marriage, especially when you add ministry to your family schedule. Create parameters with your spouse of the time you will spend on your Core commitments. For as much time as you put into Core, create equal time for your spouse, family, and self. Seek out hobbies and couple relationships outside of ministry to ensure that your life and conversations don't constantly rotate around the same people and topic. This will help create a solid balance for everyone involved.

HOLY ORDERS

I have met some of the most on-fire priests, brothers, and religious sisters while serving in the Life Teen movement. I have also met some who are burned out and overworked as well. I once met a priest at our Catholic Youth Ministry Convention who was, well, skeptical about Life Teen. He approached the Life Teen Training Convention with a "prove it" mentality and felt forced to attend and start "one more thing" at his parish. By the end of the week, he shared how the Convention reminded him of his vocational call and was renewed simply by being surrounded by people who loved God, took time for prayer and discernment, and desired to live out their faith and lead teens closer to Christ.

All priest and religious have a primary vocation to their Bride, the Church, and every Bride wants and needs a healthy spouse. Christ knew that, as a Bridegroom, He must model what a spiritually, mentally, and physically healthy spouse looks like. He modeled surrender, fasting, and prayer and He removed Himself from the crowds when things were just too noisy and chaotic. He was compassionate and forgiving, and He desired to heal those who were in sin and despair. He sought the help of His apostles and sent them out two-by-two to fulfill God's mission. He kept His focus on His Bride, the Church, and never took His eyes off of her.

Whether you are a priest or religious or you are a Core Member working alongside them, we must do everything we can to keep our brothers and sisters spiritually, physically, and mentally healthy. Keeping the vocation of priesthood and religious life primary is something we must pray through and support together to make certain our teens see that all vocations are full of joy!

SINGLE PEOPLE ARE NOT EXEMPT

Although being single is a state of life and not a vocation, I cannot ignore the majority of the men and women who serve on Core Teams. I'm just going to put this out there: being single does not mean that you should be giving more time than other Core Members because you don't have a husband, wife, or children. You are called to discern if you are called to marriage, religious life, holy orders, single, or consecrated life. "Come and See" retreats at a convent or seminary provide opportunities to see what religious life and the priesthood are like. The same is true for friendships and dating. Make time to explore, in a holy way, what vocation God is calling you to.

Other Core Members should not be your primary community. Seek out relationships both inside and outside your church community. You are strong in your faith, and God needs you to evangelize more than just your parish community. This includes your family, your friends, coworkers, and the guy you order coffee from every day. As much as your Core Team is like your family, it is important to be independent of that family and be a witness of faith to more than your Catholic community.

THE CORE OF THE MATTER:

1. Ministry is designed to flow out of our primary vocation. Would you say that your ministry as a Core Member achieves this? Why or why not?

_____

_____

_____

_____

_____

2. What is one thing that you can do to ensure that you keep your vocation primary at all times?

_____

_____

_____

_____

_____

WHAT ARE YOUR GIFTS?

- -

I always love asking people, "What's the one job you would NEVER want to do?" Some answer doctor, trash collector, *Dirty Jobs* host, or President of the United States. Regardless of the reasons why we wouldn't want a specific job, it's probably safe to say that we either don't have the giftedness to pull it off or it just isn't something we are passionate about.

Many of us have natural abilities to do certain things like typing, painting, or mathematics. These natural gifts are given to us at birth and are strengthened throughout our lifetime. Our spiritual gifts are imparted to us by the Holy Spirit and strengthened within us for the glory of God. However, there is a difference between natural gifts and spiritual gifts, and how we use both to serve and glorify God is something worth exploring.

NATURAL GIFTS

I know it may seem prideful, but I need you to honestly list the things you naturally do well. How did you discover that you had these gifts? What have you done over the span of your life to improve these gifts? All of us have gifts or things we can do that we have never had to consciously work at being good at. These are our natural gifts and, for the most part, we share them with the world. Nevertheless, many gifts go unnoticed out of shyness or the missed opportunity to strengthen the gift through lessons, practice, or study. For example, you might have a great voice that only the shower curtain gets to hear, but then one day you are singing at church and someone compliments your voice. Do you blush and disregard the compliment or do you believe that you have a gift to share?

I want you to think of a childhood gift that you always wanted: a specific toy, a puppy, or an electronic. Imagine if you received this gift and you never opened it. First, I have to say, poor puppy. Secondly, why? It was meant to be opened and used and since you never opened or played with it, the giver of the gift was denied seeing the happiness it brought you. All gifts, spiritual or natural, are given to us from God. Accepting your gifts and humbly sharing them is a gift to the giver as much as the receiver. Please accept your gifts and allow them to be seen, heard, and experienced in your family, parish, and community.

SPIRITUAL GIFTS

There are multiple passages in the Bible that speak of the spiritual gifts that God has imparted to His people. Romans 12:3-8 speaks of the gifts of prophesy, ministry, and teaching and how we must do all "in exhortation [...] in generosity [...] with diligence [...] and with cheerfulness." 1 Corinthians 12:1-31 reminds us that there are "many kinds of spiritual gifts but the same Spirit" and that we are one body in Christ, though many parts. 1 Ephesians 4:4-8, 11-16 adds, "grace was given to each of us according to the measure of Christ's gift."

All three of these Scriptures list various spiritual gifts God has given to the Church. I urge you to read, reflect, discover, and accept the spiritual gifts God has imparted to you. Acceptance is often the most difficult part of receiving a spiritual gift, because once we accept it, much is expected. No spiritual gift is given to us to hoard or hide. It is given to us to be revealed through our bodies: our mouths, our eyes, our lips, our hands, and our voices.

1 Corinthians 12:24-31 reminds us that some spiritual gifts feel greater than others in the eyes of the world; however,

in the eyes of God, all are equally necessary to build the body of Christ. We must "eagerly desire the greater gifts" while accepting each spiritual gift as it is given. Grasping at the gift got two people in the Garden of Eden in a bit of trouble. God will give you the spiritual gift you need when the Church needs it to be revealed.

SHARING GIFTS

1 Peter 4:10 says, "As each one has received a gift, use it to serve one another as good stewards of God's varied grace." God entrusts gifts to us so we might serve others as good stewards of our time, talent, and treasure. When a Core Team serves one another *and* the teens fully aware of the natural and spiritual gifts they bring to the ministry, 1 Peter 4:11 is fully lived:

> "Whoever preaches, let it be with the words of God; whoever serves, let it be with the strength that God supplies, so that in all things God may be glorified through Jesus Christ, to whom belong glory and dominion forever and ever. Amen."

It is important that we are able to see the giftedness in ourselves as much as in our brothers and sisters on the Core Team. If we are insecure in our personal giftedness, feelings of jealousy can rise to the surface. There is no room for jealousy or envy on a Core Team. We should always seek to see each other through God's eyes and desire that everyone share his or her gifts.

Be careful not to typecast a Core Member by his or her natural or spiritual gifts. Being a Core Member is a very safe environment in which to discover new gifts that you weren't aware you had or gifts you want to increase. Simply because a Core Member is great at editing movies for Life Nights doesn't mean that's all he or she can do. Be willing to stretch yourself and try new things. There will never be a more supportive audience to succeed or fail in front of again.

THE CORE OF THE MATTER:

1. Assess your greatest gifts and choose two or three to share aloud with the group (remember false humility is true pride).

_____

_____

_____

_____

2. Spend some time affirming one another, proclaiming and praising the gifts of your fellow Core Members.

_____

_____

_____

_____

_____

COMING TOGETHER AS A TEAM

I have been a part of a lot of teams in my lifetime: soccer, volleyball, dance, and drill team. In the Church I have been on retreat teams, confirmation teams, leadership teams, and Diocesan youth rally teams. Whether it was a sports or church team, each had common characteristics that made us come together as a team. All characteristics were necessary and most were unspoken, but all helped us create a family bond that helped us succeed in our team GOOOOOOOOOOALS (sorry for the soccer pun – had to do it).

- **Clearly define your vision and mission.** Having a clear vision and mission statement keeps your team on track. Proverbs 29:18 says, "Where there is no vision, the people will perish." Be able to articulate and define this vision so that your entire ministry stays focused on what God has called it to be, not what sounds fun in the moment.

- **Know your Core Team expectations.** All Core Members should know what is expected of them and be held accountable by more than just the youth minister. A Core that self regulates is a Core that truly cares about one another. This includes being on time, following through on your commitments, and praying for and with one another.

- **All Core Members have a voice.** Everyone on the Core Team has a voice. Every idea is listened to, there's always an ear to hear, and people feel free to share their thoughts and opinions. This will allow for a more creative and open environment and build unity and trust.

- **Have fun together.** Create times to hang out and get to know one another (and spouses/children). This fosters a family relationship and allows trust to be built with one another. Go bowling, attend a homecoming game together, or have a potluck dinner. It doesn't really matter what you do; just have fun doing it.

- **Honest evaluation is valuable.** Every Life Night should end with a time for evaluating the night. The point is to continually seek the best for the teens, and sometime that means criticism and honest evaluation. This should be of high value to the Core Team and never done with the intent to hurt anyone. This honest evaluation will make your ministry and your team stronger and better.

- **Affirmation is valued even more.** Affirming one another is very important in a ministry that is open to so much spiritual attack. When you notice a Core Member doing something well, affirm them in a genuine way and seek to lift one another up, not down.

- **No gossiping.** There is no room for gossip, especially on a Core Team. The quickest way to destroy relationships and trust is gossip about one another or the teens and their families. Establish whatever "no tolerance" rule for gossiping you want, but establish a rule and hold one another accountable.

- **Pray.** Pray with, to, and for one another consistently. If possible, go on a Core Retreat once a year to stay spiritually centered as a Core Team. Spend as much time praying as you do preparing for a Life Night. Your team will be able to discern things together when you pray in this way.

- **Hold each other accountable.** Finally, remember that you represent your Core Team in whatever you do and say; so whether you are together on a Friday night or not, you remain one body in Christ. Strive for personal holiness and hold one another accountable both at church and away from church.

THE CORE OF THE MATTER:

1. Rate how your Core Team is currently doing with each of the aforementioned bullet points in this section and discuss on a scale of 1 to 10.

_____

_____

_____

_____

_____

_____

_____

_____

_____

_____

4

CORE DISCERNMENT

BY MARLO DOWDY

DISCERNMENT

No matter what role you play in Life Teen, full-time or volunteer, you are part of a missionary movement to lead teens closer to Christ. As a Core Member, the hours you put into building relationships with teens and pointing teens to Christ is a call that Christ has put in your life. Some are called for a season; others are called for a lifetime.

It is important that we continually pursue God's call to ministry in our life. We do this by intentionally discerning where He wants us to utilize the gifts, passions, and time He has given us.

Discernment is more than choosing a good option over a bad option. Discernment is a journey to live life. It is the process of making the best decisions that glorify God and lead both you and others closer to Christ. In this case, you would be discerning the choice to serve as a Core Member.

Below are questions to pray through as you begin on Core, discern your role as a part of the Core Team, and look forward into continued service each year.

It is important to take time to sit and be still before the Lord. Spend time before the Blessed Sacrament. Ask Him to walk with you through these questions. Wrestle through where God is specifically calling you to serve. If you have a spiritual director, process your answers with him or her. Schedule a time to meet with your youth minister to pray through the discernment process.

Discernment is a process. It takes time and is often more than just one hour before the Blessed Sacrament. So grab a cup of coffee and enter into conversation with your best friend, the Triune God.

> *"You shall love the Lord your God with all your heart, and with all your soul and with all your strength"* (Deuteronomy 6:5).

> *"Love God and then do what you will"* (St. Augustine).

DISCERNING BEING ON CORE

- Do I have a vibrant Eucharistic spirituality grounded in the teachings of the Church, the Sacraments, and the Word of God? Is my Catholic faith apparent in my daily living (*CCC* 255)?

- What am I passionate about? Do I have a passion to lead teens closer to Christ?

- Where is God calling me to serve and give of my time to build His Kingdom (*CCC* 898)?

- What brings me peace? When I think about being involved in youth ministry do I find God's peace?

- Community life as a part of the Core Team is more than a social club. Am I joining Core to lead teens closer to Christ as part of a missionary movement? Or is my main motive to be a part of a group (*CCC* 2045)?

- Do I desire to live out the Core Spirituality and mission of Life Teen?

- Am I able to commit the time and energy required to lead teens closer to Christ as a Core Member?

- Do I aspire to grow as a minister and develop my abilities through prayer, training, and conferences (Ephesians 4:15,16)?

DISCERNING YOUR ROLE ON CORE

- What gifts do I bring to the community (1 Peter 4:10)? Are there gifts/talents I can use to reach teens? Music? Art? Sports? How can these gifts be used during Edge or Life Teen? In relational ministry at school or in the community?

- Is there a need that is not being met? Hospitality? Environment? AV/Technical? Promotion? Web/Media? How can I assist with this need?

- What area can I grow in this year? Giving a talk or testimony? Improving my gift to lead a small group? Assist with retreat planning?

DISCERNING ANOTHER YEAR ON CORE

- Where is God calling me to serve and give of my time? Has my passion shifted?

- How have I grown in my relationship with Christ?

- Do I regularly attend Core planning meetings, prayer gatherings, and Life Teen events?

- Am I reaching out to teens in and out of my parish as an active part of our relational ministry goals?

- As a Core Member, am I honoring my vocation (single life, marriage, religious life)?

- How am I using and growing in my gifts as a Core Member?

- At Mass and Life Teen gatherings/events, do I model what it means to be hospitable?

- Am I prepared for ministry on a regular basis? Each Life Night as well as retreats and events?

- Do I invite other adults into ministry? Am I still passionate about leading teens closer to Christ? Do I desire for others to be a part of this ministry?

- Are there any special issues or concerns happening in my life that would have an impact on my commitment and involvement in the youth ministry in the coming year (relationships, other commitments, etc.)?

THE CORE OF THE MATTER:

1. Take some time to discern.

_____

_____

_____

_____

_____

_____

_____

_____

_____

_____

_____

_____

_____

_____

5

CORE AUTHENTICITY

BY RANDY RAUS

BE
REAL

- -

One vital posture of heart that we must always strive to maintain in our ministry with teens is being authentic. They need to know that those who lead them are, at times, just as weak as they are, as prone to sin, and also need someone to point them in the right way. Teens don't need a polished, smiling, perfect Core Member. They need a fellow "sinner" who makes mistakes, too, and will walk with them as a companion in all the messiness that is life. They need someone who is not perfect but strives daily for holiness.

Authenticity is derived from the Greek word *authentikos*, which literally means "real."

In our world today, consumers are gravitating toward brands that they sense are true and genuine. Hunger for what is authentic is all around us. You can see it in the way that millions are drawn to mission-driven products. It is extremely important that we take notice of this trend and establish, in our parish, the authenticity that so defined the early Church. They were real with each other. They had true fellowship. They confessed sins together. They received healing together. They prayed with one another. They opened their homes to each other.

Teens desire this type of community: a place of belonging, a place of intimacy, and a place of honesty in a dishonest world. Youth group should be a place where they can be real — scars and all. Teens deserve an environment where they can truly work on their faith and develop from being cultural Catholics into practicing Catholics.

Honestly, it starts with us. We need to set the stage for this type of authenticity. We need to make it a goal for our ministry to and with teens.

Here are a few ways you can make sure you are being authentic in ministry:

- When presenting in front of a group of teens, don't try to be cool or someone you are not, simply be yourself. Teens can sense a fake a mile away; they just want you to be yourself.

- In small groups, be open to sharing areas you have healed from in your life and faith journey. Give teens a real perspective, and also give them hope that through God they can find healing and growth.

- When a teen asks you a question about the Church or God that you don't know the answer to, be real and tell them you don't know and that you will find the answer and get back to them.

THE CORE OF THE MATTER:

1. Write down three or four adjectives the teens in your parish might use to describe you. Share with the group and humbly ask your fellow Core Members if these are consistent with their perception.

_____

_____

_____

_____

_____

_____

_____

_____

_____

_____

_____

_____

6

CORE RESPONSIBILITY

BY PAM ZIMMERMAN

WHAT AM I
SAYING "YES" TO?

- -

You've said "yes" to being a Core Member, but what exactly did you say yes to? What is going to be expected of you from your pastor, your youth minister, and the teens? That can be a source of anxiety for everyone if it is not defined. Being a Core Member is more than just showing up for the Life Night and talking with the teens. We are asked to share our time and our gifts, our spirituality and our heart for God with the teens, their parents, the youth minister, other Core Members and even the parish at large. Let's look at some of the specific ways this will happen.

MASS – THE HEART OF THE MINISTRY

As Core Members, it is very important that we attend the parish Mass that the teens will be attending, whether it is the Mass right before the Life Night or another designated parish Mass. It is hard to encourage weekly attendance at Mass from teens if they feel it is not important to celebrate together. Welcoming teens and their parents as they arrive for Mass and knowing them by name is a wonderful way to show how important it is that they are there. Core Members also have a responsibility to set examples of appropriate behavior for the teens during Mass as well. This means no gum chewing, no talking to those around us, no using our cell phones; but, above all, it means that we exemplify full, conscious, and active participation in the celebration of the Mass.

We can also be called to serve the teens and the community during the Mass. We already mentioned being greeters as people come into the church; by serving in the ministries for the Liturgy (lectors, ushers, and Eucharistic ministers) we show the teens that we are part of the larger parish community.

LIFE NIGHTS – WE'RE IN THIS TOGETHER

As Core Members, we are called not only to attend the Life Nights but to also plan and assist in presenting them. As a Core Member in my parish, this is the most challenging and time consuming for me. Our team is assigned a Life Night and it is our responsibility to plan the presentation: snacks, environment, executing skits, assigning who will do the Proclaim, and who will lead the prayer. This requires a lot of extra meetings and time, but we take our job very seriously. Not all of our Life Nights have been the type of "success" we envisioned (some have been very forgettable!) but the teens know the love we have for them is in the effort we put forth.

Being a Core Member takes a commitment from everyone on the ministry team. If we have a Core Member whose "yes" is more a "maybe," everyone suffers. By being on the Core Team we have said to the youth minister, the other Core Members, and the teens that we will serve with our very best. If a Core Member is only there for the Life Night and doesn't help set up or tear down, if they don't make the Core and planning meetings, it can be damaging to the Core's cohesiveness. Being a Core Member is being in ministry – we are not just volunteers. It makes a difference; we must be committed.

RETREATS – GETTING AWAY TOGETHER

Retreats are an important part of a youth ministry program. Getting away from the "daily obligations" that everyone has can provide an opportunity to encounter Jesus. As a Core Member, retreats are great fun, definitely lots of work, and weekends away from home with little sleep. Our retreats take over two months of intense planning and meetings to get everything ready and everyone focused on the retreat theme and schedule, but it is worth it. For me, being a chaperone in a cabin in the woods on a not-so-comfortable mattress, hoping we don't blow a fuse with all of the blow dryers, trekking down the hill to the bathrooms, or getting them to quiet down so I can get some sleep provides time for laughing and sharing with each other.

As Core Members, we should have many opportunities to be in relationship with the teens in our program. Some will be obvious, as in small groups at a Life Night and on a retreat. But there are other times we can take the extra effort to reach out and let a teen know we care. Attending their plays, concerts, sporting events, or visiting campuses,to share lunch (if the school permits) are great ways to be a presence in their world.

We also need to take advantage of other opportunities to be involved in parish ministries and to be an advocate for the youth ministry program. Being involved in other ministries, asking for prayers from the prayer team, or getting teen volunteers to help at the parish picnic allows the parish community to be involved in your ministry and helps teens understand that they too are part of the parish life.

THE CORE OF THE MATTER:

1. What are some of the obstacles to the commitment needed to be a successful Core Member?

_____

_____

_____

_____

2. In what specific areas are we a successful Core Team, and where can we improve?

_____

_____

_____

_____

3. Discuss one or two areas in your own life that saying "yes" to God has required you to say "no" to something else.

_____

_____

_____

7

CORE CATHOLICISM

BY MARK HART

AT THE CORE

I sat stunned in the back of the room. I was in shock. "Did he just say that?" I asked myself in utter disbelief.

I had been asked to speak at a multi-parish teen retreat (in a state that will go unnamed). During this particular session a local priest was present and had agreed to answer teen questions about the faith. I had joyfully handed over the microphone and retreated to the back of the room to listen, as I love to learn and jump at the chance to grow in knowledge.

At this point there are a few things I should probably tell you about myself:

1. I hate romantic comedies but love my wife.

2. I have a love for all things Mac (the computers, not the makeup).

3. I have a fear of snakes...and clowns.

More importantly, though:

1. I have an ardent, deeply rooted respect for the priesthood (Sirach 7:29-31).

2. I can be a little overzealous when it comes to the honor and privilege of sharing God's truth.

3. I take assaults against Mother Church very personally.

Now that we've covered that, let's resume the story.

Teens had begun the "Q and A" with the typical questions. Questions about Reconciliation, questions about the severity of popular sins, questions about who was or wasn't/is or isn't going to hell, etc. One teen, however, asked a question of supreme importance. It was not about Church discipline. It was doctrinal. It was basic Theology 101, but with an undertone of cynicism and disbelief on his part. It was one of those prime moments in youth ministry, one where he just lobbed up a softball and you smiled, knowing that the batter could take it out of the park if he just leaned into the Church's wisdom.

The priest, the spokesman for the Church in this moment, in a collar and holding the microphone said, *"Well, I'll tell you what the Church teaches...but..."*

And that's when it happened. That's when the priest said it.

He said the three little words that caused me a whole new patch of gray hair – the three little words that can cause a world of problems for any well-intentioned youth minister or, worse yet, an impressionable and hungry young teenage soul.

He said, *"...in my opinion..."*

To be clear, it wasn't wrong for Father to have an opinion any more than it is for me to have one. Opinions are important. Opinions are valid because we feel them. Opinions, however, are not truth. Opinions are not, necessarily, even rooted in truth. Opinions are just that – they are opinions; they are useful (sometimes) and painful (often).

The way that the priest phrased and framed his response, though, was completely inappropriate. Saying "Well, I'll tell you what the Church teaches, but in my opinion..." in a catechetical moment, in a public setting was not only irresponsible, it was manipulative and selfish. It was betrayal of both Mother (Church) and Bride (of Christ).

Imagine, just for a moment, that the teen had asked me a question about my marriage or about the Sacrament, in general, and I as a married man replied, "Well, I'll tell you what my wife wants to hear...but here's what I really think."

In that moment, if I've got the microphone, I'm not only using my voice, I am **the voice** of the Church. I don't care if it's in a cabin in the woods or behind an ambo – in the mind of the adolescent, new to the faith and wading through the often-conflicting messages of the world and the Church, there is little difference. The teens' faith lives are still finding roots. Their loyalties are still being tested and their trust still being built.

In an effort to honor Father, I allowed him to finish and leave the room before I resumed the session and "re-explained" the Church's official position in such a way that left absolutely no doubt as to where Mother Church stands on the matter. Remember #3 up top? *Ya, nobody better be talkin' bad 'bout our Mama!* Now, this is not to pick on that particular priest. I can only name a handful of times since I first became a Core Member (almost 20 years ago) that a priest has said or done something like this in my presence. Our priests are good men – great men – valiant warriors for truth and harbingers of Christ's glory.

No, most of the time when I hear those three little words, they come from a random Core Member or a lost parent. I've heard them uttered in small groups. I've heard them uttered when meeting with a disgruntled parent at a coffee shop. I've heard them used to cover a multitude of situations in which people outright disagreed with Church

Teaching and wanted to alleviate all guilt in teaching their young people otherwise.

We are called, however, to raise our children in the truth. Actually, we're called to "drill truth into them" (Deuteronomy 6:4-9). We are called to support parents as the primary catechists (*CCC* 2223), again **reinforcing the truth of God's revelation,** safeguarded and offered to us by Mother Church.

There is no room for personal opinions, euphemistic language, watered-down and vanilla theology or private agendas. Raising our next generation in the faith is a privilege. It is a grace and a gift from God. Being a good **Catholic** parent takes prayer and study. Being a solid **Catholic** Core Member takes prayer and study. Good intentions aren't enough – not when formation is coming through the lens of the secular media.

I'm not under the impression that anyone who is reading this book has a hard time with the Church or her guardianship of objective truth. This is preaching to the choir (quite literally, for those of you who are also in music ministry). But, if we don't remind our Core Members, parents, and others of the divinity of our Church – beyond just her humanity – we run the risk of unraveling from within.

I pray you never have to hear those three little words in a ministry setting. I pray, too, that you'll never have to leave a room, seek out the person who said them, and have a conversation like I was forced to have many years ago with that well-intentioned, but misguided, priest. I offered mercy. He responded indignantly. And while we didn't see eye to eye (and possibly never will), it's comforting to know that Mother Church still loves him deeply ... and that he knows never to talk about my Mama in that way again.

As you've no doubt noticed, this is something I'm quite passionate about. It's a heavy responsibility and great privilege to speak on behalf of Mother Church. So, let's get practical and go over some important "reminders" for the next time you offer a teaching or a witness at an Edge or Life Night.

PRACTICAL REMINDERS WHEN GIVING A TEACHING

- Use the Proclaim teaching outlines (in your Edge Semester Planning Guide and Life Teen Curriculum Guide) as a guide. Don't feel the need to re-invent the wheel. You might need to pare down some of the content as we try to give you even more than you'd need. Don't shy away from tough topics, either. Pray hard. Prepare well and give the teens the fullness of truth – they can handle it; they desire it.

- Practice your teaching out loud for others or on a video you can watch of yourself. The more aware you become of your idiosyncrasies and habits, the more you can eliminate any that might be distracting.

- Pay attention to your time. Have a stopwatch running on your phone or a timekeeper sitting near the front. If you can't make your points within ten minutes, you're probably trying to do too much.

- Be sure your fellow Core Members are sitting amongst the teens and scattered throughout the room to help you. If teens begin talking to one another or at you, let the other Core Members deal with the distraction(s) so as not to interrupt your flow or your thought process.

- Be sure your teaching is relevant to a teenager's life. Build in examples and correlations that won't leave them asking or wondering about how it relates to them. Additionally, give them something tangible to "do" or think about or apply to their life that night or the next day to live out what the Church is saying.

- Be sure to make eye contact with everyone in the room. Don't talk "just" to the teens in the front or the back. Vary your attention and your eye contact as you go to ensure everyone feels "connected" to you as the presenter.

- If you use notes, try to have them reduced to an outline form. Avoid reading your talk. Boil down your main points to words or short phrases on a paper to signal to you what your next point is, should you lose your place.

- Try to avoid asking questions to the group that will invite digression. If you want to be interactive and allow them to respond to things, it's up to you to frame a question that requires more than a "yes/no" answer; ensure that they raise their hand and limit side conversations. The microphone is in your hand; you're the pilot and they are the passengers, do not relinquish control of the room or you'll crash land.

- If you're not naturally "funny," don't try to be. It's more important that you are authentic – the teens respond to the real you, not a character. The person greeting them at the door or leading a small group has to be the same person they see up front talking. Find ways to affirm them during your talk, as well; letting them see your heart will earn you credibility and give your message greater effectiveness.

- End the talk with a brief prayer whenever possible, before you transition into the Break portion of the night.

PRACTICAL REMINDERS WHEN OFFERING A WITNESS

- Create an outline for what you will share and in what order. While the witness should be from your heart and guided by the Spirit, an outline helps ensure the point is made, tempers emotion, and alleviates unnecessary tangents. Set a time limit and stick to it at all costs.

- Glorify God, not yourself. The point of a witness is not to show people how great you are, but rather, how great God is and how He is at work in your life. If your witness points more toward you or others than it does to the greatness of God, it needs to be reworked or eliminated altogether.

- Pay attention to details, sharing only those that matter. Often, when sharing more personal things, we have a tendency to use two thousand words when two hundred would suffice. Concentrate on the most important details and tend more toward brevity than exhaustive background information – the teens will take far more from it.

- When sharing a story of conversion, do not inadvertently "empower" teens to sin. For instance, stating, "All through college I was drunk, but I met Jesus after I graduated and…" can unwittingly leave certain teens feeling that they can live immoral, intemperate lives during their undergraduate years so long as they straighten up soon after. While you don't want to be dishonest, you should also give great care to how you phrase certain things when sharing. Focus more on the greatness of God and His mercy than on the details or depravity of personal sin.

- Never share a struggle you're currently "battling." Sharing personal or difficult challenges are fine, but only once you've conquered or "gotten ahead" of them, not behaviors or addictions that still have daily "power" over you.

- Tie your witness into their walk with Christ. Perhaps they haven't been through exactly what you have, but the lesson you learned and shared about should be able to be applied to their own lives (under different circumstances). Be sure to "connect the dots" for them to take something from your experiences.

- Point them back to the Sacraments. If you share about past sin(s) be sure to point out that you availed yourself of God's forgiveness in Reconciliation. If you share about a struggle with prayer or doubt about God's presence, talk about what a blessing Mass and Adoration have become in your life. Whatever you focus on, point to how the Sacraments have helped solve your issue or comfort you during times of struggle.

ADDITIONAL CATHOLIC RESOURCES TO HELP YOU

You don't have to be a theologian to minister to teenagers. That being said, it's important that you continue to study and increase your own ongoing catechetical formation. The more you know the more you can share. Below is a brief list of some solid Catholic resources that I recommend often to souls serving in the youth ministry trenches.

I'd encourage you to get some of these resources to have on the shelf in the youth ministry office or, better yet, on your own shelf or nightstand at home. These books will not only expand your knowledge but will help you in "framing" different conversations and discussions with the teens of your parish.

Catholic Study Bible
People are always asking me what the "best" translation

of Bible is to use when working with teens. The two I recommend are the RSV–Catholic Edition or the NAB (New American Bible). The RSV-CE is the best translation for study, closest to the original texts, and is the one cross-referenced in our *Catechism*. The RSV-CE put out by Ignatius Press is my personal favorite. Additionally, the Ignatius Catholic Bible study series by Dr. Scott Hahn and Curtis Mitch is positively first-rate for daily study and Mass preparation.

I also like using the NAB with teens, which is the translation we use for our Life Teen Catholic Teen Bible. The NAB is also the translation we hear at Mass (here in the U.S.) and the one teens are most familiar with.

The Catechism of the Catholic Church
Obviously, it is essential to have a copy of the *Catechism* available to further unpack all our Church teaches and safeguards as truth. In addition to the original, there are several other versions of the *Catechism* that are quite useful in teen catechesis.

The *Compendium to the Catechism* is a great resource. The *YouCat* is pretty well written, too, and easy for teens to understand. Finally, *The Essential Catholic Catechism* by Alan Schreck is a great tool to understand the teachings in more conversational language.

Additional Resources
It is impossible to narrow down the additional helpful resources into one list, but here are a handful that I refer to often that are great for anyone who didn't major in Theology or who wants easily digestible, solidly Catholic works to refer to:

• *Catholic Christianity* – Peter Kreeft

• *Bible Basics for Catholics* – Dr. John Bergsma

- *Catholic Bible Dictionary* – Dr. Scott Hahn

- *Fundamentals of the Faith* – Peter Kreeft

- *Essential Catholic Survival Guide* – The Staff of Catholic Answers

- *Common Sense 101: An Introduction to G.K. Chesterton* – Dale Ahlquist

- *A Compact History of the Catholic Church* – Alan Schreck

- *Theology for Beginners* – Frank Sheed

- *Because God is Real* – Peter Kreeft

THE CORE OF THE MATTER:

1. What are the greatest dangers in allowing personal opinions into youth ministry discussions?

_____

_____

_____

_____

_____

_____

2. What would be an acceptable course of action for a Core Member if they were struggling with a Church teaching? Define a protocol within the Core Team that will both ensure fidelity to the Church and to the pastor.

_____

_____

_____

_____

_____

_____

8

CORE SKILLS

BY TRICIA TEMBREULL

GATHER – PROCLAIM – BREAK – SEND (GPBS)

- -

Every Mass has four major movements: the gathering or entrance, the Liturgy of the Word, the Liturgy of the Eucharist, and the recession or sending forth. Each movement calls us to use all our senses to participate fully, consciously, and actively in the celebration: sound, sight, smell, taste, and touch. This model for celebration has been effective for centuries, so why reinvent the wheel when it comes to Life Nights?

At the start of each Life Night we Gather the teens, creating a welcoming and loving environment where community can be fostered. As the night moves from icebreakers and skits into the Proclaim of the night, the theme or topic is brought to life, complete with *Catechism* and Scripture references. Just as the Body and Blood of Christ are broken and shared, we do the same with the Break portion of Life Night. Teens are encouraged to break open the topic of the night by sharing their understanding, lives, and experiences, asking questions, and seeking answers amidst a community of trust. Finally, at the end of the Life Night, we Send them forth in prayer, often challenging them in a specific way to be living witnesses of their Catholic faith.

This model of youth ministry allows teens to make their faith their own. Combined with a youth Mass, teen's lives are forever changed as truth is proclaimed through Word, sacrament, and the actions of their Core and peers. Let's take a closer look at each movement of a Life Night so you can begin to envision how you can make your Life Nights come to life.

GATHER

There are two aspects of the Gather we want to discuss: pre-gather and gather time. Most teens make up their mind before they enter the doors of the church whether they are going to Life Night or not. So the question becomes, "what have you done prior to their arrival at church to get them to come to Life Night?"

Pre-Gather

Consider the publicity and communication of your Life Night calendar. What forms of communication are you using to inform teens about what is happening at Life Teen: emails, text messages, bulletin announcements, phone calls, flyers, websites, etc.? What forms of relational ministry take place from week to week to form new relationships with teens who have never been to your church, let alone a Life Night: campus visits, sporting events, Life Teen Club on school campuses, school events, etc.? How does Core interact with the teens at Mass (and not just youth Mass, all the Masses at your parish on a given weekend): do you introduce yourself to families, invite teens to come to Life Teen, attend other Masses? Finally, how are teens invited to attend a Life Night before or after the youth Mass: tickets to get in the door, personal invitation, announcements, etc.? These are all pre-gather things to consider prior to when the teens walk in the door of a Life Night.

Gather Time

Gather game time has three major movements within it: environment, hospitality, and community building.

1. **Environment** - The first things teens will notice when they enter a Life Night is the environment. You do not have to spend a lot of money on environment, but do something to immediately set a tone for the night. Here are a few aspects of environment you want to consider:

- Music (live or recorded)
- Sets and Backdrops
- Lighting
- Seating set up
- Video Loops (Life Teen or Edge)
- Sound
- Audio Visual set up
- Banners
- Costumes for Core
- Prayer space

Be creative and have fun with environment. If you are looking for cheap ways to create environment, check out the blogs on CatholicYouthMinistry.com.

2. **Hospitality** - Every Core Team evaluation at the close of a Life Night should start with this question: Did every teen feel loved tonight? If this is accomplished each week, we are serving the Church as Christ called us to. Hospitality is key to the Gather of each night.

3. **Community Building** - In every Life Teen Curriculum Guide, we provide a variety of ideas for Gather activities. Everything from videos to skits, games, contests, and more. You can either use these as they are written or adapt them to fit the needs of your parish teens. The point of these Gather activities is to draw teens into the focus of the night, break them out of their comfort zones, build community, and allow them to have fun.

PROCLAIM

Just as the Word of God is proclaimed at Mass, the message of the Life Night is proclaimed during this section. And just as Scripture is meant to teach and instruct the Church, Life Night teachings are meant to speak truth on catechetical teachings, cultural issues, and social situations that teens face in their daily walk. Life Night Proclaims should never be boring, void of passion, or impersonal. Instead, they should be taught with conviction, personal belief, and understanding, and bursting with personal testimony.

Proclaims should be taught by a variety of people including Core Members, priests, youth ministers, outside speakers, parents, and teens (for witnesses and testimonies). Keep the talk within 10 minutes, since teen's attention spans are limited. It does not have to be one person talking for 10 minutes straight. There are a number of ways you can teach the Proclaim of the night with originality, including:

- Tag team talks
- Debates
- Pre-made videos
- Skits
- Personal witnesses or testimonies
- Questions and answers
- Monologues
- Dialogues
- Methods in which teens are involved in the execution of teachings

In planning your Proclaim, take into consideration the needs of your teens and the resources of your parish. For example, the teaching outline for each night is filled with more information than a typical teenager can absorb during a 10 minute talk. But by giving you, the presenter, more than enough information, the outline can help you create an engaging and informative presentation.

Preparing a Proclaim
Any effective Proclaim must do three things:

1. Communicate the truth of the Church.

2. Persuade the teens that this truth is good news.

3. Be interesting and entertaining.

It is impossible to communicate and persuade effectively without entertaining teens. Keeping teens captivated is essential to communicate your message and its value. Basically, you need to keep their attention.

Listening is hard work, especially at Life Nights where teens attend weekly and have many distractions around them. In a catechetical talk, entertaining doesn't mean making your audience laugh or distracting them from the topic. Instead, it's about helping them stay focused on and interested in what you have to say. There are no rules that apply always and everywhere. But the following principles work almost all of the time:

- Talk rather than read
- Stand up
- Use visual aids such as props
- Move around
- Vary the pitch of your voice
- Speak loudly, clearly, and confidently
- Make eye contact with the teens
- Use humor
- Get into character (possibly use costumes)
- Add impact with audience participation opportunities.
- Be real and tell your story
- Focus on the main point
- Finish your talk within the time limit
- Summarize your talk at the beginning and again at the end
- Notice your teens and respond to their needs
- Emulate excellent speakers

(For more practical reminders on how to give a teaching and a witness, reread Core Catholicism starting on page 65.)

BREAK

I don't know about you, but my favorite part of school was recess. Taking a break in the middle of school to run around, release all my energy, be loud, and spend time with friends was what I needed after what felt like hours of listening to my teacher go on and on or taking a test I prayed I passed. Well, the Break section of a Life Night often creates the same sense of excitement for teens. This is the time of the night when teens can move around, build community, and process everything that they just heard or experienced in the Proclaim. It is also the place where the most depth can come to fruition.

The Break section of a Life Night should accomplish the following:

1. Break open the topic so teens can apply it to their daily lives.

2. Break down personal and spiritual walls.

3. Build up trust within the community.

This is accomplished in a variety of styles and formats including:

- Small group discussions
- Large group discussions
- Partner sharing
- Questionnaires
- Journaling
- Silent reflection
- Guided meditations
- Scripture verse reflections

This is the one part of the Life Night that can cause Core anxiety, especially if teens are not participating or being unruly. Getting teens to take part in a small group discussion, skit, or even quiet journaling can be tricky when trust is not established. The key to any Break activity is to build up trust by starting with a common activity or question and then going to greater depth. Teens will not share intimate, personal moments of their lives with outsiders, so take the first few minutes to pray and get to know one another, hopefully creating an environment that fosters safety and a freedom to share.

(For more about small groups, check out the "Why Small Groups" section found starting on page 88.)

SEND

My family was one of those families that stayed at Mass until the final note was played on the church organ. My brother stood twitching to leave the second Father passed our pew, but my dad just shot him "that" look. When he got his license and we would go to Mass without my parents, he would leave after we received communion – what my brother called "half time." I, being the perfect child of God, would just walk back to our pew and kneel while he waited in the car. I could say I did this because I fully understood the grace received in the final blessing or that I wanted to take time and contemplate the Body and Blood of Christ present at that moment within me, but I would be lying. I did it to aggravate my brother. I was the youngest and it was my job.

So often the Life Night Send is the most unplanned, rushed part of the night. The Gather and Proclaim go longer than planned so the Break and Send get cut short or cut altogether. When well planned and given sufficient time, a Life Night Send can be the most meaningful part of the night. The purpose of the Send is to end the night in prayer and empower the teens to live out the message proclaimed at Life Night in their daily walk. Just as in the closing blessing at Mass Father invokes the grace of God upon his congregation, sending us forth in peace to love and serve the Lord, a Life Night Send should empower the teens to go forth in a similar manner. Without that blessing, our Mass experience is incomplete. When a Send is cut short or sometimes omitted, the Life Night will be incomplete as well.

In addition to rushing, cutting short, or even cutting out your Send, you might find your Send becoming predictable or stale. The Send is meant to introduce teens to a variety of spiritual disciplines and traditions, so try new things as well as things to which your teens respond well when bringing them into prayer with the Lord. Don't get stuck doing Adoration weekly or simply praying prayer intentions. Introduce your teens to these disciplines and devotions:

- The Divine Mercy Chaplet
- The Rosary
- Liturgy of the Hours
- *Lectio Divina*
- Novenas
- Silence
- Fasting (not just a Lenten practice; pick a day during the week)
- Service
- Offertory
- Intercession
- Adoration
- Prayer cards
- Prayer partner/accountability
- One-A-Days (daily challenges and prayer practices)

WHY SMALL GROUPS?

- -

We have all been there before: the filthy, frigid gym floors welcome our slumped over posture and the halogen lights buzz overhead – teens are avoiding eye contact with us at all costs. Oh, the dreaded small group! But fear not, *small groups are not about having all the right answers; they're about asking all the right questions*. Read that again and let it sink in. Small groups are a combination of relational ministry and catechesis. Relational ministry makes sense since small groups are a great opportunity for teens to share their feelings, attitudes, beliefs, disbeliefs, and lives with us. Catechesis happens when we take teens deeper into the teaching and make the faith both personal and transformational.

This is why we offer teens small group opportunities. They are there to engage teens in solid, Christ-centered discussions and give them the freedom to ask questions that require an internal response. Small groups challenge them to process the topic of the night, and they create a safe environment that allows everyone to feel valued. The more we understand how to lead a small group and remove the fears surrounding them, the more we can lead teens closer to Christ.

Here are a few reminders to keep your focus and keep your small groups moving:

What Is Your Desired Goal?
The question you must ask yourself before every small group is, "What do I want my teens to walk away with from our time together?" Your goal might be that every teen is

able to answer the question, "How does my faith change me?" or "What is one way I can commit to being a disciple in my school, family, or social relationships?" Knowing your desired goal for the small group time will provide freedom for the Spirit to move and allow the entire time to feel more conversational and less forced.

Engage Teens in Solid, Christ-Centered Discussions

Most small group leaders will start their small group time with the first question on the list provided by the youth minister. This is not the way to "engage" teens in a dialogue. How would you feel if you walked into an adult group and were suddenly asked, "The Holy Spirit transformed the apostles so that they could transform the world. How do you need to be transformed so that you could transform your life, your family, your friends?" The conversation would feel abrupt, causing you to shut down. Small groups are the same. You need to ease teens into a conversation by asking non-threatening questions. First show them that you care about them and then lead to the questions you desire.

Ask Questions that Require an Internal Response

The biggest mistake we make in small groups is missing opportunities to take the conversation deeper. Ask follow-up questions that are not on the list when a teen gives you a cliché answer without much thought. Push the teens to dig a bit deeper by asking, "So what makes you say that?" or "How would you explain that answer to your non-Catholic friends?" You have permission to go off script and make them think about why they answered the way they did. Teens know how to get out of a conversation by giving us the answers we want; however, what we really want is for the teens to commit to their faith and be able to articulate our Creed with understanding and conviction.

Challenge Teens to Process the Topic of the Night

We need to challenge teens so they can articulate their faith with confidence. In small groups you might need to create a debate or start an argument to get the dialogue moving and allow teens to process the topic of the night on a personal level. Be willing to ask questions like, "What would you say to someone who wouldn't agree with you?" or "Why do you think the Church speaks so passionately against or for this?" Be prepared for teens to not agree with Church teachings, but be willing to provide answers or follow up with them if you do not have the answers to their questions.

Create a Safe Environment that Allows Everyone to Feel Valued

Life Nights, in general, should have a code of confidentiality. Small groups should be a place of intimacy, trust, and honesty, and they must provide an opportunity for every teen to participate and share without the fear of gossip, bullying, or any social media ramifications.

SMALL GROUPS IN ACTION

The role of a facilitator is a very unique role; as Core, you have the official title of "facilitator." Your job, simply put, is to lead the teens while keeping the conversation focused. More often than not, teens will try to get the group off task by asking questions unrelated to the topic. The struggle is keeping the teens on task and the conversation flowing. Here are a few suggestions on how to start and lead the group discussion.

Starting a Small Group

When starting a small group, be sure to do the following two things so everyone feels welcome:

1. **Introductions** - Have everyone introduce themselves in small group. You can ask them to say their grade, school, and whatever additional piece of information you might desire to ask. As a Core Member, remember their names

so you can call on them in case teens are not sharing or there is a discipline issue.

2. Prayer - Once everyone is introduced, lead an opening prayer. If you would like a teen to do so, invite them to lead it, but warn them ahead of time so they are not uncomfortable or nervous. Invite the Holy Spirit to be present and in control of your time together.

Starting the Conversation
Starting a conversation isn't as uncomfortable as you think. Here are a few techniques that can work to get them talking:

1. **"I Say Whip It"** - A great way to get the conversation started is to do what is called a small group "whip." This is where you whip around in a circle and get a one-word response that will lead into a deeper conversation. It allows every teen to share a non-threatening response and gives you permission to go deeper with a follow-up question. The following are a few examples of a "whip" question:

- On a scale of 1 to 10, how close are you to your parents?

- If you were a patron saint, what would you be known for?

- What is the first thing you notice about a person? (This is especially funny if there is a new teen in at the night and you can follow it up with, "Is that what you noticed about me?")

- What is the most important quality for a friend to have?

The key is to create a "whip" question that works with the conversation you want to enter into, so think before you ask.

2. **Prepared Witness** - On very rare occasions you might want to ask a teen to think about a tough question in advance so that they are ready to answer first in the small group. On difficult topics, this is a great way for teens to open up a bit easier. Use a teen that you know will not dominate the conversation and will take the responsibility seriously.

3. **Processing Time** - Some teens need time to process their answer and are unable to just blurt out a response. As the small group time begins, you might want to pass out some paper or a journal to have them respond to a question and think it through for a few minutes. Then come back and invite teens to share.

4. **Pictures or Visuals** - Providing some visual aides such as images, photos, or magazines can help start a conversation. Place some in the center of the room and ask them to find an image that describes how they feel about what they just heard in the Proclaim or a question you asked.

   Have each teen explain whey they chose the image they did and let the conversation move from there.

5. **Conversation Starters** - Sometimes the best questions to ask to break the ice in a small group are not necessarily related to the topic. For example, "What food can you absolutely not stand to eat?" or "Do you floss your teeth?" There are a ton of "Table Talk" games or conversation starter websites out there, so check a few of them out.

KEEPING THE CONVERSATION GOING

The reason we are unable to keep teens talking or maintain control of a small group has more to do with personalities than techniques. Here is a detailed list of different teen personalities you *will* have at one time or another in small groups and some suggestions on how to engage them in the conversation.

Quiet Teens
- Ask these teens by name to answer specific questions.

- Speak to quieter teens prior to small group and let them know that you will be asking them to contribute to a question that you might or might not choose to give them in advance. Tell them that you know they have a lot to give and you wish everyone could hear his or her input.

- Give them time to process the answer to a question. Many times teens are quiet because they have not been given enough time to process their answer and cannot come up with an answer quickly.

- Allow teens to journal on a couple questions and then have them share their answers. This can help these teens process as well as contribute to the conversation with depth and thought.

Talkative Teens
- You don't really need tips to get talkative teens to talk; you need tips to get them to be quiet.

- Ask them to help lead the group questions. This helps give them a chance to hear others first before answering.

- Call on people by name instead of asking if "anyone" would like to share.

- Position yourself next to this person so that you can tap him/her on the knee to let them know when it is time to move on.

- Allow talkative teens to start a conversation and then

throw a beanbag or item to another person to keep the conversation going. By simply holding the bag in their hand they know that they are limited on time.

- Speak to this teen prior to sitting down in small group and explain that you value their input but that you really want everyone to have equal time to share.

Tangent Stealers
- These teens add a lot of energy to a small group but often make it hard to stay on track. They are often the comedians of the group and will crack jokes just to throw the facilitator off track and get attention from the group.

- Always be prepared to pull the conversation back in and, if necessary, just stop the conversation and tell the group that you can wait till they are done. When they see that you are frustrated they will often quiet down.

- If the tangent can be tied back into the conversation, use it to your advantage. Sometimes this is possible and the tangent allows for the conversation to really get going.

- If the tangent is a serious switch to an issue one teen is going through, discern if that is where God is calling the group to go. Be willing and ready to go with the Spirit.

Emotional Teens
- These teens steal the show because everything makes them cry or brings up a serious emotional issue for them.

- Emotional teens need a lot of attention and are often a dominating personality in small groups.

- Be compassionate but, at the same time, offer to talk with them at the end of the night about their issue or situation. Offer to pray with them during or after the large group prays at the Send of the night.

Debater

- These teens will question Church teaching because they simply like to debate. They desire things to be proven and will challenge you in small groups, which will allow you to really help teens take ownership of their faith.

- In all reality, they will make you and your teens stronger Catholics so embrace their questions, but keep the conversation focused and do not allow them to control the small group.

- Ask questions like, "Does anyone else feel the same way?" to create a group discussion rather than an individual debate.

- If an understanding or consensus does not get reached by the end of small group time, follow up during the week with a few Scripture and Catechism references for your small group. Close the time with prayer, asking for the group's hearts to be open to the mystery of our faith.

Flirts

- Often teens are in youth ministry more for social reasons than for spiritual growth. They go from teen to teen in the youth group for dance dates or a new boyfriend or girlfriend, and cause drama when they break up.

- In small groups these teens can be diverted by facilitator placement as well as small group separation (how you break up your groups in the first place).

- If some of your teens are in relationships, do not put them with their boy/girlfriend. If they are seeking a relationship, be aware of who they are interested in and sit between them or move the teens away from one another if they are an issue.

Uninterested

- There are some teens who are there because their parents dropped them off and made them come. These teens need additional relational ministry attention so they enjoy being at a Life Night.

- Spend time talking with them prior to the beginning of the night, and ask your youth minister to place them in your small group once a relationship is established until they get to know more teens and Core.

- Follow up over the next few days with a call, note, or even a visit to a play, sports event, or whatever they are involved in to show interest in their lives. Don't be forceful or invasive, but let them know you care.

- Accept whatever they give you in small group, but still challenge them based on what you know about them and their comfort zone.

AFTER THE SMALL GROUP

The best part of a small group is that it opens the door to an ongoing conversation and relationship. The end of the Life Night does not mean the end of the conversation between you and the teens. Often follow-ups need to take place about an issue or question that came up during the night. Here are some thing to consider after the small group ends and they are called to "go forth to love and serve the Lord."

Unanswered Questions

You might run into a situation in a small group where teens ask a question about a topic completely unrelated to the discussion. If a question is too difficult to answer in a short amount of time or they are asking for information you just don't know or have, follow up with them before the next Life Night to show that you were listening and desire them to know and trust Christ and His Church.

Sacraments
In a small group, teens might bring up sins that they have not reconciled with God. Encourage them to meet you at Reconciliation when your parish offers it. Sometimes they just need to go with someone, and the fastest way to lead teens closer to Christ is walking with them to the Eucharist or standing with them in a Reconciliation line.

Counseling Referral
During your time as a Core Member, you will have to discuss sensitive and personal topics like divorce, homosexuality, suicide, cutting, etc. Many of these nights will prompt teens to share things in their lives that might require immediate attention. Some nights will require conversations with parents and counselor referrals. Be prepared by having available a list of counselors to whom you can refer teens and their parents.

Prayer Support
If a teen shares something rather difficult or personal, offer to pray with them at the close of the night. It is a way to show compassion and support and allow for the conversation to go deeper if the teen trusts you. It takes the relationship to a more personal level and shows intentional listening and care.

Child Protective Services (CPS)
If child abuse or neglect is reported in a small group and you are a mandated reporter (review list of mandated reporters from your diocesan guidelines), report the concern and inform the youth minister and/or clergy of your report so they can also follow reporting procedures. If you are not a mandated reporter, inform your youth minister and/or clergy and they will place the report based on the information you have gathered.

THE CORE OF THE MATTER:

1. In addition to the tips and insights found here, what tips do you find most effective for leading a small group?

_____

_____

_____

_____

_____

_____

_____

_____

_____

_____

_____

_____

_____

TEEN DISCIPLINE

- -

Disciplines are a set of rules or methods that many of our teens do not know, just as they don't know the maker of the rules: Jesus Christ. And as we all know, Christ didn't come to create more rules; He came to remind us of one very important rule: to love one another. As Core Members, we must strive to be disciples who teach teens to follow Christ's example of love, compassion, and mercy.

Here are a few important reminders about how to best discipline teens:

- **There are no problem teens … just teens with problems.** Those problems typically create the discipline situations, so take time to get to the underlying issue that a teen is going through verses just reacting.

- **All teens are different, so treat them differently.** Treat each teen differently by recognizing that each of their upbringings, cultures, ages, educations, and gender will greatly influence how you handle the discipline situation.

- **Leave your problems at the door.** We, as ministers, will have bad days and it will affect how we react to teens. As much as possible, leave your problems at the door when you arrive to a Life Night.

- **Proactive discipline verses reactive discipline.** Teens need structure from the start, and informing teens on a weekly basis how they are all called to respect one another and the leaders throughout the Life or Edge Night is a great way to prevent discipline issues.

- **Don't assume anything.** Get the full story from multiple witnesses and not just the people involved. There will always be multiple versions of a story. If Core is involved, you want to stand behind your fellow youth ministers; but keep in mind that teens need to be heard, so ask Core to be quiet and listen while a teen explains his/her side of the story.

- **Door openers verses door slammers.** One important listening skill to use when teens are upset or in conflict is using door openers as opposed door slammers. Door openers are open-ended responses that don't imply judgment. Ask questions like, "I'm interested in what you are saying" or "That sounds important to you" or "Do you want to talk about it?" These questions and statements will encourage an open listening situation.

- **Love the teen; hate the behavior.** Teens, even in the midst of a bad situation, need to be affirmed and loved. They need to know that, no matter what, you will love them. This is where understanding the teen and his or her background is so important. They might be reacting to abuse or neglect at home rather than a peer or leader in the youth group. Discipline the action and not the player.

- **Two minutes, two hours, two days.** When a discipline situation arises, it is good to take time to calm down before disciplining a teen. Give yourself two minutes before you speak for two reasons: to not say anything you regret while calming down and to not freak teens out. Silence is a powerful tool in heated situations. If you are not calm after two minutes, place the teen in their parent's care and say you will call them when you are ready to talk. This can be either two hours or longer. If you need to consult the pastor because the situation involves his input, take two days before getting back with the teen and his or her parent(s).

- **Meet the parents.** You know the old saying, "It takes a village to raise a child?" Well, you are just a village member. It is important to build a relationship with parents prior to a discipline situation occurring. This way, the first conversation you have isn't a difficult one. Affirm the teens and be in good communication with parents about what you are doing from week to week so that if an issue ever comes up, they trust that you handled it with love, truth, and compassion.

- **Follow up.** At the end of the night or mid-week, be sure to check in with the teen to show that there are no hard feelings and to be sure that they understand your expectations of being a part of the ministry. If apologies are necessary, be sure that they take place between the persons involved. Also make sure they understand that you forgive them and that they are loved.

THE CORE OF THE MATTER:

1. Spend some time in prayer for the teens that bring about the most amount of frustration or discord and pray for them, as a Team, daily.

_____

_____

_____

_____

_____

_____

_____

_____

_____

_____

_____

_____

_____

9

CORE OUTREACH

BY JOE CHERNOWSKI

RELATIONAL MINISTRY 101

- -

"Relational ministry!" "Go outside your comfort zone!" "Love those teens!" You'll hear these sorts of things over and over at Life Teen training events. Hopefully your youth minister harps on it, and it has been mingled throughout this resource in various ways.

When you get right down to it, what is relational ministry? It's a lot of different things and it's one thing: loving the teens. It is manifest in literally countless ways, and the pages that follow will try to break it open for you in a practical way. To really get at the heart of what we're talking about regarding relational ministry: it's basically you relating to the teens as individual persons that you individually care about. Rather than just seeing a sea of faces each Sunday night, along with a blur of nametags and trendy shoes, you see individuals that you genuinely know and care about and that you are in contact with beyond just Sunday nights. This is one of the key elements of Life Teen – we aren't simply adults present at events to enable the teens to gather. We are called and challenged to journey with the teens – to be a reliable presence in their lives.

Core outreach is a huge, broad area but it all is simplified into the posture of heart of each of the individual Core Members. This component of being a Core Member won't look anything like how other Core Members at your parish live it out – your personality, your passion, and your desire to love these teens and bring them to Christ will shape your relationships with the teens you encounter.

Probably the least understood part about being a Core

Member is the aspect we call relational ministry. This aspect of the Core Member's role impacts all components of being involved in Life Teen at your parish. Relational ministry is boiled down to just a few words: love the teens. That sounds really simple and really easy – or maybe it doesn't – but when it comes down to it, relational ministry is simple but not necessarily easy.

Relational ministry plays a large part in the heart of Life Teen. Maybe in the past we've seen social nights consist of rolling out a basketball or faith formation relying a great deal on classroom time and lecturing or workbooks. Life Teen asks more of the adults involved. Relational ministry is about us showing the teens that we love them – individually and personally.

Imagine walking into a party of 60 or 70 people where you know a few people, but not many. You've met the hosts of the party a couple times, but not so much where they'll go out of their way to make you feel welcome. In fact, they have a hard time remembering your name when you walk in. Maybe the people you know are already circled up having laughs that you feel left out of. This probably isn't a party you want to stay long at.

Now imagine you go to a party and, right when you walk in, the hosts call you by name, ask you how things are going, check up on your recent soccer game, and intentionally work to make people feel welcome and part of the group. That's not only a party I'd want to be at, but I'd be asking about when the next one is before I leave. We want Life Teen at your parish to be the party that teens know they are welcome at – a place where they know people care about them personally, and a place they can feel at home.

Relational ministry is the fancy way of saying "get to know the teens personally." Invest in them, beyond the 90 minutes of the Life Night. If they miss a week or two, send an email or a Facebook message letting them know you've missed them. If they've got a big game coming up, grab the youth minister or another Core Member and head out to cheer them on. Challenge them in their prayer lives. Offer to work on a prayer partnership to pray for each other's intentions each week.

Before giving any talks and before leading any small groups, the job of a Core Member is to simply love the teens that walk in. No matter why the teens are there, or what their attitude seems to be, we just need to love them for who they are and where they are in their faith. There are so many components to this that a comprehensive list is impossible. Your personality will shape how you become a relational minister.

One thing we absolutely need to keep in mind regarding relational ministry is that it isn't about us. We want to build relationships with teens, we want to get to know the teens, we want to challenge the teens, we want to journey with the teens, but all of this is in the hope of leading the teens to Christ, not to ourselves. We aren't getting to know the teens because we want more friends – this is an intentional relationship. That doesn't mean it isn't sincere and that we won't build up a natural trust. It is an honor to be present at the wedding of former teens, to see their children, to visit them at their jobs – essentially, to be part of their lives after they graduate from high school.

One thing we need to keep in mind is that teens aren't an island, and they aren't isolated. Teens have parents, siblings, grandparents, neighbors, etc. There's a good chance that (hopefully) they already have strong adult presences in their lives. We are not taking the place of parents. In fact, in order to really be able to journey with and help the teens through challenges that come along in life, it is very helpful to get to know the parents and families of teens. This can be as simple as just saying hi when the teen gets picked up on Sunday nights or chatting with the parents when you go to his or her soccer game.

Probably the greatest example of relational ministry you can see is that of Christ on the road to Emmaus, in the Gospel of Luke. Christ joins up with a few disciples, walks with them, listens to them, shares truth with them, and then leads them to the Eucharist. It is the whole picture, all in one Gospel chapter. That is exactly how we are called to live out our call to relational ministry, though the specifics may be different. We will be joining up with teens on their walk in faith. We will listen to their stories, listen to their perspective, and listen to their hearts. We will boldly and gently correct and teach the Truth – with our lives and with our words. We will lead the teens, ultimately, to the Eucharist.

THE CORE OF THE MATTER:

1. Discuss as a group why relational ministry is so foundationally important to a successful youth ministry program.

2. How does relational ministry make a Core Member's job easier on a Sunday night?

_____

_____

_____

_____

_____

_____

_____

_____

_____

_____

_____

_____

OUTREACH

We were going to a high school football game. Somehow, I had talked a Core Member into going with me. But it honestly felt like we were walking into that pit of snakes Indiana Jones finds himself in *Indiana Jones and the Raiders of the Lost Ark*. It all sounded great in theory. Walk in, high five some kids we knew, hang out and chat, cheer for the home team, make our rounds, and head out. As soon as we walked through the stadium gate, however, we knew it just wasn't going to be that easy. Teens were all over the place – of course, what would one expect at a high school football game? Honestly, the large majority of teens were not familiar to us, and they completely ignored us. But then something strange happened. When we first found a few teens we knew, they were really excited to see us. Guys and girls, upperclass and underclass, they were all happy to see us there, and they were excited that we had stepped into "their" world. Parents were also glad to see us and chat for a bit. What started out as an awesome concept quickly turned into something fearful, but it then became evident that the night was a victory.

Giving up every single Sunday night is already a big commitment, and for that we, along with your youth minister, cannot thank you enough. But to truly dive into being the Core Member that your parish and the teens need, we're asking you to give more. We're asking you not to just invest in Sunday nights, or in Life Teen or in youth ministry – but to invest in teens. To truly invest in someone you've got to get to know them and know what's happening in their lives, their successes and their failures. I realize that takes a great deal of time – time you might feel that you don't have.

Being a Core Member isn't something that we're asking of you on a whim. It isn't something to do because you're bored, or just want a place to fit in. It may fit into those things, but the Core Members that are the best – the Core Members that make the biggest differences in the lives of teens – are those that have a sense of mission and of purpose. More than being a part of the great community of the Core Team and giving of their time on Sundays, being part of Core is being a missionary and acting with a purpose greater than yourself. Relational ministry is something that needs to be intentional, needs to be done with a missionary heart, and we need to keep in mind the purpose of leading the teens to Christ, not to ourselves.

What makes outreach so vital is a bit of perspective. It is great if we are welcoming and inviting at Life Night. It can mean a lot to reach out and ask a teen personally if they will be coming to the next retreat or to camp this summer. But all of that is our zone. That's us inviting and welcoming the teens in the church and to events that the church is running or organizing. When we go to a football game or a choir concert, we are stepping out of our perceived "safe zone" and into the world of the teen. When we bring ice cream sandwiches to teens at the end of a school day, we are firmly in their territory, and the teens know this. They know how uncomfortable that can be for us, and they truly appreciate us going out of our way to walk into their world.

That's why outreach is so crucial to really loving the teens and walking with them. We're not just asking the teens to be a part of the life of the Church and a part of our life when we're at the "safe" church events. We are reaching out to be a part of their lives and we are stepping into their world. That's what outreach means, and that's probably the hardest part of being a Core Member – to put ourselves in these sometimes uncomfortable situations for the sake of loving our teens.

Honestly, there just isn't any choice in the matter. Our Life Teen ministries need to be outreaching to our teens. There are a myriad of ways to do it: visiting schools for lunches, going to choir concerts, hitting up the plays and musicals, getting to soccer and basketball and football games, chaperoning dances, and going to graduations. Really, the list is as long as you are creative about it. But honestly, please, get creative and schedule relational ministry into your weekly calendar. Youth ministers should be prioritizing this regularly, and Core Members should also have goals of periodically attending different events for teens. Perhaps at a Core meeting you can come up with a realistic strategy or goal for individual Core Members, and encourage follow-through by asking for reactions at other Core meetings.

This seems like an "extra" or an "add on," but, in reality, it is just as crucial as Sunday night Life Nights. By reaching out to teens, we are showing that we care, personally and individually, about them, and this will give us the opportunity to share faith and to ultimately lead them to the Eucharist.

THE CORE OF THE MATTER:

1. Discuss the elements of outreach that make you the most uncomfortable. Why?

_____

_____

_____

_____

_____

_____

2. As a Core, brainstorm both events and opportunities that you can take in pairs, or as a group, to further what you're doing at the parish.

_____

_____

_____

_____

_____

_____

HOSPITALITY

In order to really be able to embrace relational ministry, you need to embrace the awkward. Let's be honest: whenever an adult walks up to a teen and tries to strike up a conversation, it's just awkward.

Let's take a step back. First and foremost, before we get to the grand plans of our Gather, Proclaim, Break, and Send portions of our Life Night, many teens will have already made their judgments about Life Teen. Is this place full of lame activities, or is it a place where they can feel welcomed and a part of something? Are we willing to put ourselves out there in hopes of being Christ's instrument or do we want to stay comfortable? Those questions go hand in hand.

I remember leading a one day Confirmation Retreat at a new parish a few years back. I had a team of five juniors and seniors that I hardly knew, and 44 tenth graders that I didn't know at all. I walked into the building, feeling like I was going to blow those teens away. They were going to love me, they were all going to love Jesus, and they were going to think this new youth ministry at their parish was the greatest thing going. Then I walked into the room, and honestly, I wanted to walk right out. It is flat out intimidating to walk into a room of high school students that don't know you and have hopes of impacting them that day.

That retreat had its victories and losses – there were some who jumped all into what our youth ministry had to offer and some that really felt like that day was the beginning of a turnaround in their life. Of course there were also some who could barely remember that day happened. That's the reality of relational ministry and of youth ministry.

So much of youth ministry's success is the willingness of the Core Team to go outside its comfort zone and really focus on giving Sunday nights to the teens, rather than hanging out with the Core Members they know well already. It is awesome when a Core Team is a tight-knit community – that's a good model for the teens – but what we sometimes had to do at my parish was to huddle up before the Life Night, say a prayer, and then tell all the Core Members, "I love you, I know you love me, I know you love each other, but we're giving these next 90 minutes 100 percent to those teens. So we'll talk to each other again in an hour and a half. Go love on them teens."

Being hospitable to teens at a Life night can be done in all sorts of ways. Have dedicated greeters at the door, name tags that already have the teens' names on them, activities that Core Members can immediately invite teens to participate in and then become engaged with. Here's a not-so-novel idea: food. All of us, when offered free food, are much more likely to attend a function. Don't just throw up a folding table and put pizza on it; spend a little time and have a little bit of a spread. Maybe have bowls of chips and candy already on tables. Have a dessert table with cookies or homemade brownies.

When the teens walk in, they shouldn't be ignored; they shouldn't just be expected to find something to do themselves and they should never sit alone. There are so many simple ways to truly welcome the teens dynamically. It just takes some desire to put in the preparation, work, and commitment at the actual Life Night. Hospitality is a crucial element because it gives off that first impression. Every Sunday you might have the opportunity to meet new teens and truly give them a welcoming experience. Beyond the initial welcoming experience, if we care about and are in relationship with the teens that are already active, we will want to go that extra mile to welcome and embrace the familiar faces as they walk in.

The hospitality present at Life Nights and other Life Teen functions sets the table and opens the door to all sorts of opportunities we should be hoping for. It creates those chances for real relational ministry by showing that extra effort and enthusiasm our teens deserve. A first impression can take a relationship a long way. Be willing to go outside of your comfort zone and feel awkward when approaching a conversation with a teen. It might be the only conversation you ever have with them. Or it may turn into an awesome relationship that helps you both along your faith journey and both closer to the Eucharist.

THE CORE OF THE MATTER:

1. How would you currently rate the hospitality that exists within your parish?

_____

_____

_____

_____

2. How about within your youth ministry programs?

_____

_____

_____

_____

3. What are some practical ways that you can improve hospitality at the youth group and at the parish?

_____

_____

_____

_____

PERSONAL INVITATION

- -

Think back to when you were a child, and you received an invitation to a friend's birthday party. An envelope with your name and address, with a fun card inside that had all the details of the party; it also was handwritten. It was fun, it was personal, and you felt excited to be included and a part of things. Juxtapose that image with today's parties and the dreaded Facebook invite. It's probable that the host didn't even know they invited you; they just invited all of their "friends." It's not personal, and rarely are we excited to receive that party invite. Sure, there's the odd "private" party invite on Facebook, but how often do we get all sorts of random invitations, we hardly know the people involved, and now we're getting all sorts of alerts and reminders for this event we don't really want anything to do with?

Is the way you invite and welcome like that Facebook party invite? Is it just more clutter and yelling and screaming mixed in with the rest of the yelling and screaming of our modern world? Are your teens just a number you want to be able to report to the pastor, or do they know they matter individually to you? Do they feel personally invited and welcomed by you and other Core Members?

This personal invitation cannot be understated. Which party are you more likely to attend: the one with the handwritten card sent to you with a phone number for an RSVP or the impersonal Facebook event? I know I would prioritize the personal invites – I probably know the host better, know that I matter to them, and recognize that they personally want me to attend instead of just wanting to have a certain number of guests.

Call this whatever you want – promotion, marketing, hyping, announcing – but Core Members need to have a strategy of personally inviting the teens of your parish and need to consider that each teen should somehow feel special by this invitation. We want the teens to know that it was a specific effort to invite them. Have a Core meeting where you spend time writing postcards. Or maybe you split the list of teens up into phone lists for Core Members to call over the course of a week leading up to the semester kick-off. There are many approaches, but the goal is to have each teen in the parish feel personally invited and that the invitation is worth their time for a response.

Past the initial invite of the beginning of the year kick-off or the major retreat event, how do we continue to personally invite consistently? It gets a little trickier, because it probably isn't reasonable to expect your Core Team to write out hundreds of postcards or make dozens of phone calls each week. But there are things the Core can do to continue the theme of personal invitation, and it stems directly off of relational ministry, discussed earlier this chapter. When we've built those relationships, when we know the teens well as individuals, we have a greater ability to reach out.

When a teen misses Life Night a few weeks in a row, give them a call, shoot over a text, or send a personal Facebook message – not to nag them, but to let him or her know "Hey, I've missed you. Hope all is well! It'd be great to hear how soccer is going this coming Sunday night." Quick, simple, and potentially powerful. This sort of message tells a teen they are an individual person who was missed specifically. It reminds the teen that they have a personal relationship with the Core Member and that the Core Member remembers what is going on in the life of the teen. This is the sort of personal invite that people want to respond to because it shows real care, yet it only takes a few seconds.

This is an example of why we need to be in relationship with the parents and families of the teens, and not just teens themselves. The parents need to have the goals of relational ministry spelled out to them so that when their son or daughter receives that text message or email inviting them to an event or checking up on how marching band is, they know who it is from and why it is coming.

This personal invite is also evidence of a personal relationship with the teens, and it helps the teens in numerous ways. It gives them the space to share what's going on in their lives with you. It reminds them of a friendly presence at the parish. It allows them, in turn, to invite you into what is going on in their world. It opens up communication for the teen to ask you to pray for them for certain situations in their life. Most of all, it can strengthen your relationship with that teen, giving you more of a right to be heard when the opportunities to share the faith arise. Leading the teens to the Eucharist is the end goal of all of these ministerial relationships.

THE CORE OF THE MATTER:

1. Name some places in your community where your Core Team would have the opportunity to personally invite teens to the parish.

_____

_____

_____

2. Share stories of when you've offered a personal invitation and it has gone well.

_____

_____

_____

_____

3. What can the youth minister do to help you be more successful in your outreach efforts to teenagers?

_____

_____

_____

_____

10

CORE INVITATION

BY ERIC PORTEOUS

HELP WANTED: INVITING OTHERS TO BE ON CORE

As a youth minister for nine years, one of my greatest struggles was recruiting Core Members. I tried just about everything: begging, free food, bribes. I just needed adults on fire for their Catholic faith that were willing to mentor teenagers. Was that too much to ask?

But for every one Core Member I recruited, I probably had twenty conversations that went like this:

> "Hi! My name is Eric, and I'm the youth minister here. How would you like to work with teens as a part of our Core Team?"

> "Umm...Yeah...No."

That's why it's so great that you're reading this book. You said "yes." You're one of the five percent, and for that I'm sure your youth minister is eternally grateful. But we know there are more of you out there, and we need your help.

Your youth minister is only one person, and unless they somehow learn to bilocate, they can only effectively recruit a limited number of adults to serve on the Core Team. He or she needs you to bring others into the mission of leading teens closer to Christ. If you're up for the challenge, here are three important questions to ask yourself when recruiting others to be on Core:

- **Who do you know?** Two of the most important criteria for any Core Member are that they love Jesus (and the

Church) and they love teens. Do you know anyone who fits this mold? If so, let your youth minister know so he or she can ask them to be a part of the Core Team. Better yet, ask them yourself. There are few things as effective as personally inviting someone to join you on a mission that you've been called to.

• **What have you experienced as a Core Member?** As I travel around and meet Core Members across the world, one common thing I hear from so many is: "I knew I was going to serve the teens, but I never realized how much I'd get back."

No matter how long you've been a part of the Core Team, hopefully it has meant a great deal to you. While you've no doubt given a lot of time and energy, I'm sure that God has blessed you immensely too.

Share your experience as a Core Member with other adults as you personally invite them to be a part of the team. Also, if your pastor will allow it, pray about giving a short testimony at Mass or in another setting where a large quantity of Catholics are gathered. Testimony is a powerful way to awaken the hearts of those who have not yet had the courage to say "yes."

• **Why are they needed?** Often people don't respond to something if they think that there is no need for them. As you talk with other potential Core Members, be sure to share why the teens at your parish need good and holy adults to model the faith and mentor them.

If you want to go even further, point out some of the particular gifts and talents in the person you're talking with and how they will benefit the Core Team and teens. Everyone loves being affirmed, and when they know how they can fit in, they are more likely to join.

The Core Team is the heart and soul of every youth ministry. A good one can help teens live better lives. A great one brings them closer to God who wants to transform their lives. If you want to reach more teenagers, you are going to need more Core Members. Your youth minister needs your help to identify and invite those people, but remember it's not about finding anyone to be on the Core Team. It's about finding the right ones. So share the mission, share the joys, share the heart of what you do as a Core Member with anyone who loves Jesus and loves teens. God is calling them, and the teens need them.

THE CORE OF THE MATTER:

1. Who do you know that would make a great Core Member?

_____

_____

2. What has been the most profound experience you have had as a Core Member?

_____

_____

_____

_____

_____

3. Why do the teens at your parish need more faithful and holy adults to serve on the Core Team?

_____

_____

_____

_____

_____

5 WAYS TO BE A CONTAGIOUS CORE TEAM

- -

I've always hated cold and flu season. It seems that no matter what I do, I somehow get sick:

Eat ten oranges...runny nose.

Start my day with the best herbal tea out there...sore throat.

Cover myself in every winter coat I own...fever.

And, of course, we all know that when you get sick the first thing people say to you is, "Oh, don't come around me. I don't want to get sick."

Ahh yes...there's nothing like that kind of warm hospitality when you're not feeling quite yourself. The flu can be contagious, and no one wants to catch something that makes him or her worse.

But, what if they could catch something that made them better?

What if they contracted something that allowed them to serve a demographic that desperately needs to know God's love?

What if there was a group of people whose holiness was so contagious that others just had to be a part of it?

Isn't that what the world needs? Isn't that what teenagers need? And, even though a personal invitation is a great recruiting strategy, perhaps the best way to encourage other adults to join the Core Team is to have a contagious spirit. Here are five ways your Core Team can be more contagious:

1. **Pray together.** Prayer is at the heart of all we do as Catholics. Without it, we are disconnected from God, and yet, with prayer, anything is possible. As a Core Team, it is imperative to pray together. It's not enough to just come together to minister to teens. Everything must be directed toward God, otherwise you risk only leading teens closer to yourself. Be sure to pray as a team. People will not only be more attracted to your ministry, but God will bless it abundantly.

2. **Play as a team.** Youth ministry is supposed to be fun, but too often it can be easy to get caught up in the "work" of ministry and lose that sense of joy. But, the last time I checked, most people don't get excited to be a part of something where everyone is straight-faced and "taking care of business." Laugh. Joke around. Play. This spirit of joy will definitely lead others to think, "Hmmm...they are so happy. I want to be a part of that."

3. **Humble yourselves.** During my years as a youth minister, my Core Team adopted the motto, "We Go," which translated meant, "It's not about ego; it's about we go." Ultimately this meant that there was no role too big or too small because every role was for the greater glory of God. In a world where people often focus on themselves first, who wouldn't want to be a part of a team that put aside their personal egos for the greater good?

4. **United you stand.** The 1980 U.S. Men's Hockey Team is known for their shocking win over the Soviet Union and eventually winning the gold medal. Most of us probably know the story and were inspired by their hard work and

dedication to their mission, but what else was inspiring about them? They didn't just look at themselves as a team. They looked at themselves as a family. It's that kind of unity that people want to be a part of. As a Core Team, it is vital to come together, trust each other, and have each other's back. That kind of unity has a way of rubbing off on others.

5. **Exercise your passion.** Imagine if you played on a football team and no one wanted to win. You probably wouldn't do too well, and you probably wouldn't inspire a whole lot of people. As a Core Team, it's not enough to simply go through the motions. You must be passionate about leading teens closer to Christ; when others see this passion, they will naturally want to be a part of your team.

These are just five simple things that you can do as a Core Team to be more contagious, but it doesn't do any good to just talk about them. They need to be lived. So get out into your parishes and communities. There are adults who haven't had the courage to answer the call to the Core Team. You've got the secret and perhaps they just need to be infected.

THE CORE OF THE MATTER:

1. If a Catholic adult wanted to serve young people, would they want to be a part of your Core Team? Why or why not?

_____

_____

_____

2. What's one way your Core Team spreads joy at your parish or in your community?

_____

3. How well do you trust your fellow Core Members?

_____

_____

_____

4. How do you share your passion for youth ministry with adults who are not on the Core Team?

_____

_____

_____

BONUS MATERIAL

- - - - - - - - - - - - - - - - - - -

FOR THOSE CORE MEMBERS WHO
SERVE ON A BASE OR HAVE MILITARY
TEENS IN THEIR YOUTH GROUP,
THIS SECTION IS FOR YOU.

CORE MEMBERS IN MILITARY COMMUNITIES

ARCHDIOCESE FOR THE MILITARY SERVICES, USA

This is the only military Archdiocese in the world created by Blessed John Paul II in 1985 to serve over 1.8 million Catholic Americans located around the world with United States Armed Forces. This includes more than 220 installations in 29 countries, patients in 153 V.A. Medical Centers, and federal employees serving outside the boundaries of the USA in 134 countries.

Different cultures, languages, viewpoints, and experiences all are opportunities to deepen your Edge and Life Teen ministry!

CORE MEMBERS ON US MILITARY INSTALLATION – TWO SCENARIOS:

1. **CONUS** (Contiguous United States, 48 states) teens going to civilian parish and/or military chapel.

2. **OCONUS** (Outside Contiguous United States) only option is the military chapel if family does not speak the native language.

- **Get involved, don't wait** – plug teens, parents, and adults in right away. Military members know how to take orders. Find out what they are passionate about, where their gifts lay, and give them a role to do. Military teens are more likely to get involved if they have a mission to accomplish and a purpose.

- **Relational Catechesis** – Military teens come because someone knows their name and genuinely cares about them. Often military catechesis is more classroom based. Engage in relational catechesis that teaches the Catholic faith in a dynamic way.

- **Partnership with surrounding parishes** – If you are in an area where military teens participate both at the military chapel and in a local parish, find ways to partner together. Join resources by hosting a joint Confirmation retreat, service project, or a community XLT Adoration gathering. Find ways to serve together and not compete.

CORE MEMBERS IN A NON-MILITARY PARISH WITH MILITARY TEENS

- **Engaging Hospitality** - Military teens either jump in and count everyone as a close friend or close themselves off and say, "why bother, this will be over with soon and I will be moving." Engage military teens in community. Introduce them to other teens. Help them feel a part of the group quickly.

- **Build Community** – It is uncertain whether military teens will be with you for 18 months or beyond 3 years. One thing is for sure, they need a community where they feel loved and have a venue to share and process the struggles of military life. From parent's deployments into war zone to seeing the area where their parent is on the news, military teens carry more burdens than any teen should.

- **Outreach Locally and Beyond** - Often, military teen's worldview and experiences are what some teens only see on TV or dream about. Find ways to use these experiences and the knowledge military have of the world to serve locally and around the globe. Partner with Catholic parishes in a foreign country, a charity overseas, host a night where military teens can share their experiences of the Catholic church in other countries and pilgrimages or service projects they've participated in.

- **Host Teens** - Pair teens up (local with military) – No one likes to feel like an outsider. And there is no one that feels stranger than a military teen that has lived in 4 different countries and attended 12 different schools in a room with teens that have lived in the same house their entire life. Look for ways to partner teens together. Have a local teens "host" a military teen to introduce them to others and show them the ropes. A local teen can assist in teaching culture and the norms of everyday life.

Notes _____

_____

_____

_____

_____

_____

_____

_____

_____

_____

_____

_____

_____

_____

_____

_____

_____

LIFETEEN.COM
CATHOLICYOUTHMINISTRY.COM